Mini

LAURENCE MEREDITH

SUTTON PUBLISHING LIMITED

Sutton Publishing Limited
Phoenix Mill · Thrupp · Stroud
Gloucestershire · GL5 2BU

First published 2001

Reprinted in 2001, 2002

Copyright © Laurence Meredith, 2001

Title page: The legend of Sir Alec Issigonis's little cars is kept alive by a growing band of enthusiasts.

British Library Cataloguing in Publication Data
A catalogue record for this book is available from the British Library.

ISBN 0-7509-27275

Typeset in 10.5/13.5 Photina.
Typesetting and origination by
Sutton Publishing Limited.
Printed and bound in England by
J.H. Haynes & Co. Ltd, Sparkford.

This book is dedicated to the memory of Alison Barrie

Acknowledgements

The author is grateful to the following without whom this book would not have been possible: John Day, Tom Holmes, Peter Day, Angelo Barbierato, Don Gregory, David Ashton, Colin Ashton, Dave Morton, Gillian Morton and John Hodge.

Contents

powerful image from Rover's publicity department in the late 1990s, this photograph is headed: 'Every boy's am'. By this time, BMW owned the company producing Minis, and all appeared to be well, but there were dark ds on the horizon which would almost, but not quite, put an end to 'every boy's dream' of owning and ing one of the world's most desirable small cars.

Introduction

Based on a pre-War German concept, designed by a Greek and built in Britain, the Mini survived in production for 41 years almost against the odds. Launched in 1959 to a most grateful British public, early cars were prone to leaking in wet weather, crudely appointed and, from a passenger's point of view, extremely noisy.

However, by comparison with many British mass-produced cars of the 1950s, the arrival of the Mini was like the discovery of an unlocked fire exit at a Young Farmers' disco. It was as a spoonful of strawberry jam in the centre of a bowl of semolina – that incomprehensibly vile substance that my generation was occasionally fed for 'pudding' at school – and British folk from all walks of life gave thanks. Inexpensive to buy and run, the Mini had many fine points. For example, the judicious use of extremely narrow squabs and backrests for the seats gave the cabin a feeling of space and, with a wheel 'at all four corners', the roadholding broke new ground in small car design.

These facets aside the Mini principally endeared itself to millions because of its size and looks. Like the Fiat 500 from Italy, Volkswagen Beetle from Germany and Citroën 2CV from France, the Mini was a chic 'cutey' with good looks, smiling 'face' and a rump that closely resembled the hips of a shapely woman.

A car that emerged from the effects of the 1956 Suez crisis, and originally intended as an inexpensi economical means of basic transport, the BMC Mini correctly became a motoring icon of the twentieth centu With comparatively good road manners, chic modern looks, and almost unlimited tuning possibilities, the sh enjoyment it gave from the driving seat would eventually endear the diminutive car to more than five mill grateful motorists.

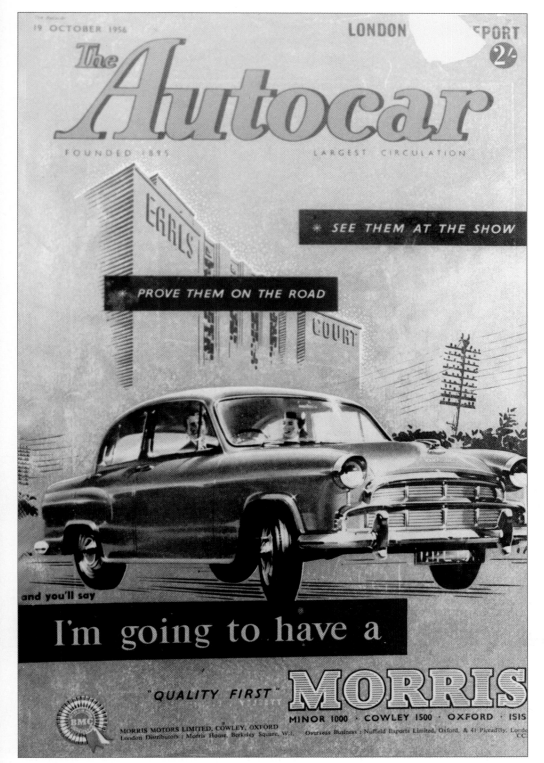

The Autocar's front cover prior to the London Motor Show, October 1956. British motor manufacturing at this time was ostensibly healthy and in full swing, but behind the scenes, there was widespread panic as a result of the Suez crisis. This led to fuel rationing in many European countries, and gave birth to a new generation of 'light cars'.

5

REVOLUTIONARY NEW BRITISH SMALL CARS

The British Motor Corporation's Austin Se7en and Morris Mini-Minor Rival Continental Designs In Respect of Passenger Accommodation, Performance/Economy and Originality; 848 c.c. Four-cylinder Water-cooled Transverse Engine, Front-Wheel Drive, Sump-located Four-speed Gearbox, All-Independent Variable-Rate Rubber Suspension and Full Four-seater Two-door Saloon Body in a Car Priced at Under £500 inclusive of p.t.

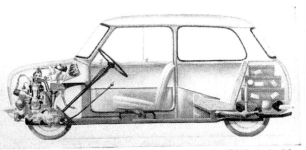

General arrangement of the new B.M.C. ADO.15 Austin Se7en and Morris Mini-Minor baby cars.

THE greatest praise and commendation must be accorded to the powers behind the British Motor Corporation for allowing Alec Issigonis and his design-team to take a clean sheet of paper when planning a revolutionary small four-seater saloon car, which is now announced, and in production, after development work and an exhaustive testing programme extending over a period of some eight years. Ever since the end of World War II MOTOR SPORT has been pressing repeatedly for fresh thinking on the part of British automobile designers and engineers, so that British cars should not lag behind Continental makes in which abolition of the propeller shaft (and in some cases of the cooling water), all-round independent suspension, horizontally-opposed cylinders and low weight have long been desirable features. In persuing this policy I left myself wide open to criticism that I was anti-British, possessed substantial investments in foreign automobile factories, was on the Wolfsburg payroll—none of which is true! All I could do in reply was to affirm that I am in control of a *motoring*, not a *political*, paper and that if and when worthwhile new cars emanated from British factories I would accord them equal publicity and praise.

This year the Triumph Herald arrived as a brilliant new model in the one-litre family-car class, with i.r.s., elimination of greasing points, many safety factors and a taxi-like turning circle, features acclaimed with enthusiasm by MOTOR SPORT, culminating in a detailed, unbiased and analytical road-test report in the July issue.

Now the British Motor Corporation has gone a step further, in a rather different class, with its completely revolutionary and eminently practical Issigonis-conceived new small car, made in two versions as the Austin Se7en and Morris Mini-Minor, but virtually to be regarded as one model technically, known as ADO.15, differences being confined to radiator grille style, colour shades and interior trim.

The General Conception

This vitally important new B.M.C. model is not only a completely fresh conception of small car design, but it is offered at a sensationally modest price. *Under these circumstances it is difficult to see how sales of Continental small cars can be maintained in this country and America.* Since the war there has developed a growing home and United States demand for cars which are " different," which embody items of specification rendering them interesting to own and comfortable and economical to drive, and if a high price, brought about by adding Import Duty to basic cost, has been involved this has not mattered to the bulk of these Continental car " fans." With the new Austin Se7en and Morris Mini-Minor costing not only far, far less than these Continental invaders but less than all other reasonably-sized British vehicles with the exception of the out-moded Ford Popular, and being essentially a practical approach to the unchangeable problems of transporting four adult persons in comfort and safety, they surely cannot fail to deal a knock-out punch to Continental-car sales, which will now presumably revert to the pre-war " drop in the bucket," kept going by a few fanatical enthusiasts for particular foreign makes and more definitely by the especial merits of, for example, air-cooling, rear-engines and low-speed power units in particular circumstances.

Admittedly the " proof of the pudding is in the eating," but from what I have seen of this new B.M.C. small car it is likely to fulfil this prediction—when it was first shown, to a select party of experts, there were certainly some who became so enthusiastic they seemed almost prepared to eat what was set before them and brief driving experience certainly confirms the maker's claim that these new " puddings " set completely revised standards of safe handling.

These Austin Se7en 850s and Morris Mini-Minor 850s also seem to belong to a new class of family vehicle—dimensionally they are very small—in fact mini—cars, but generous accommodation for four persons and the good performance to be expected from a high-compression 850 c.c. engine propelling some 11½ cwt. of motor-car makes them serious rivals of existing small cars of up to 1,200 c.c. Moreover, with tuning kits which are available from specialist sources and their revolutionary cornering power these new cars should make a great impression *amongst sports-car drivers and rally competitors.*

When I had revealed to me the intimate details of the new Issigonis design I listened with an unbiased mind to the reasons why the specification used was decided upon. I am conscious that only after an extensive road-test can an opinion be expressed as to how successful the B.M.C. has been in its effort to offer an extremely low-priced, entirely new small family car. I shall not overlook the need to take the car into slimy fields, up steep hills and through deep water splashes before bestowing praise or criticism on this sensational front-drive, transverse-engined, all-independently-sprung vehicle. I have every reason to believe that as soon as possible the B.M.C. will place a car at this paper's disposal for prolonged road-test and in the meantime I can only remark that I am exceedingly impressed with the new car after examining it carefully and driving it on a test track.

Although no manufacturer makes public the findings of the experimental department, the B.M.C. makes no secret of the fact that many experimental models were built and tested before the present specification was adopted. I believe these included a decidedly unconventional and compact engine and certainly vehicles with two-cylinder air-cooled power units and with pneumatic suspension, etc., were tested exhaustively before being discarded in favour of the present layout which, and this is significant, *although refreshingly new, does incorporate an engine and other features, such as gearbox*

ASSESSING THE STABILITY of the Morris Mini-Minor. The Editor of MOTOR SPORT hurls the little vehicle about and discovers that it hardly rolls and displays no vicious oversteer tendencies. This 180 deg. corner could be taken at 40 m.p.h. with complete equanimity.

Revered motoring 'bible' *Motor Sport* described the Mini, upon the car's launch in 1959, as 'revolutionary'. Editor Bill Boddy had nothing but praise for the Mini, and its design team headed by Issigonis. With a fearsome reputation for honesty, Boddy commented in this piece: 'This vitally important new BMC model is not only a completely fresh conception of small car design, but it is offered at a sensationally modest price. Under these circumstances it is difficult to see how sales of Continental small cars can be maintained in this country and America.'

vival of the globally famous Cooper versions in the 1990s, saw a revival in the Mini's fortunes. In many ways
e car was entirely outdated, and outclassed by modern 'superminis', but this didn't prevent healthy sales among
any enthusiasts throughout the world. Despite having undergone modernisation, this 1997 Cooper retains the
aracter and spirit of the much-loved original cars of the 1960s.

I first became interested in these British machines after watching them racing against, and beating, much more powerful cars during the early 1960s. At around this time, my late father took up rallying, mostly in Beetles with the great Bill Bengry (winner of the RAC International Rally Championship in both 1960 and 1961) but, after changing Volkswagens for Minis, winners' trophies were collected more frequently – and sit proudly on my mother's hideous 1950s sideboard to this day!

My father and his friends used to return home on a Sunday morning after a rally for breakfast, their Mini-Coopers covered in mud, occasionally bearing the deep scars of motoring battle and, as a lad, the sight of battle-torn Minis and smell of hot engine oil made a lasting impression on me.

Minis excelled in motor sport during the 1960s, both in rallying and track racing. When the British Vita racing team came to the fore in the mid-1960s and beyond, saloon car championships came alive. These cars, painted blue and white, were usually sideways, always smoking their tyres and went like hell. Incidentally, saloon car races in those days were lost and won without drivers banging into each other and depositing expensive pieces of bodywork on the track for others to pick up.

It was all a lot of fun; race meetings were held in an age when motor sport was not a public relations business. It was a sport and those who took part were

As an automotive shopping 'trolley', fast road transport, successful rally machine, giant-killer on the race trac few cars have achieved more than the humble Mini. More than 40 years after the car's official launch, thousan remain in daily use, and . . .

sportsmen. Sponsorship was minimal and companies that did spend money to gain publicity for their products were almost always connected with the motor industry.

Famous international Mini victories included Paddy Hopkirk's 1964 win on the Monte-Carlo Rally, and the infamous 1966 debacle in this event which saw the disqualification of the works cars which finished in the top three places. Incensed that such a small car – and a British one at that – could comprehensively trounce the opposition, including Citroën's best, the French organisers found against the Minis because of a minor and wholly inconsequential lighting infringement.

Their decision was outrageous, but it worked well for BMC, as the ensuing publicity in the international press made a bigger impact than a straight win without complications. In international events the Mini's supremacy was toppled at the end of the 1960s, principally by the twin-cam Ford Escort and Porsche 911. The little car, however, continued as a hugely successful competition machine in national club events, and this remains the case today.

Despite many highlights in the car's production career, though, there have been periods of abject despair. The car has frequently been blighted by appalling build quality, poor management at both middle and senior levels and insignificant sales abroad. Down four decades of production, the Mini has been available in Britain, and almost nowhere else in the world. A small number of cars were built under licence by Innocenti in Italy, and the Japanese have had a healthy interest in the car for a long while but, as for the rest of Europe and North America, the Mini is virtually unknown.

an untold number still languish in garages, their owners full of good intentions, enthusiasm and the desire to their classic British steeds returned to something approaching former glory. Thanks to the thriving classic car vement, and specialist motor industry, parts for Minis are plentiful and cheap, and the sum of the parts most lectable.

The Mini should have been considerably more successful. Responsibility for its dismal failure to capture foreign markets must be borne by managers at senior level.

Between 1945 and the present day Volkswagen have built 22 million Beetles; from 1948 to 1972 BMC produced just 2 million examples of the Morris Minor, and between 1959 and 2000, just 5 million Minis have rolled from the assembly lines – less than one third of the number of Golfs produced by VW since 1974!

A senior director of BMC in the late 1960s once told me that the Mini's designer, Alec Issigonis, always insisted on those present at company board meetings sitting, not around a table, but in the lotus position on the floor. Against a background of such lunacy, it is difficult to imagine that BMC produced cars at all.

In the mid-1960s Walt Disney produced a number of 'Herbie' films starring a VW Beetle as the principal player. Volkswagen of America co-operated wholly with Disney, and made a number of Beetles available – around 30 in all – at discounted prices. The publicity from these films had a large impact on worldwide Beetle sales, and Volkswagen made handsome capital.

By contrast the makers of the contemporary film, *The Italian Job*, starring Michael Caine, Noel Coward and a number of Mini-Coopers, approached BMC in much the

'Get in, sit down, shut up, and hang on' is a popular slogan and sentiment among Mini owners today, but many this sums up everything that is great, good, bad and indifferent about the magical little car from the fer mind of its creator, Sir Alec Issigonis.

same way as the Disney Corporation had sought the help of Volkswagen. True to form BMC refused discounts, even though the film makers required a large number of Minis for the Italian Job, the directors of the latter eventually securing their cache from a dealer in . . . Switzerland!

There were times during the 1970s, when BMC had been taken over by British Leyland, that plant workers vented social disquiet by staging a series of strikes from which no-one benefited. It was a time in the company's history that few wish to remember. After South African business supremo, Michael Edwardes, was appointed as chief executive, the company's future appeared brighter; but the Mini Metro, launched at the end of the 1970s, failed as a replacement for the venerable Mini.

Through thick and thin the Mini survived. The people who built it, largely by hand, are justifiably proud of this enduring British classic, for it remains among the world's greatest cars. This is clearly recognised by BMW, who, in producing the new Mini with 'retro' styling, have honoured a British classic that inspired a whole generation of 'super-minis' from rival manufacturers in the 1970s and beyond.

During the course of writing this book I met many people whose enthusiasm for the Mini remains undiminished. Their considerable efforts in restoring, driving and enjoying these British cars are to be warmly applauded. Only time will tell whether the new Mini will enjoy the same success and following in the years ahead.

Chronology

1952 British Motor Corporation (BMC) is formed as a result of merger between Austin and Morris. Alec Issigonis leaves the company and joins Alvis.

1955 Issigonis returns to BMC as part of a design team working on a family saloon.

1956 The Suez Crisis leads to fuel rationing in Britain and many European countries. Issigonis begins work on the design of a small, economical car.

1958 Mini prototypes are built and extensively tested without major problems.

1959 Series production of the 848cc Mini begins, and is available with Austin or Morris badging.

1960 A team of Minis is entered for the Monte-Carlo Rally, but the cars prove underpowered. Estate versions, the Austin Seven Mini Countryman and Morris-Mini Traveller, are debuted.

1961 Luxury versions of the Mini with larger boots debut, and are badged as the Riley Elf and Wolseley Hornet. Issigonis appointed Technical Director of BMC.

1962 BMC launch the 1100 saloons with hydrolastic suspension, also adopted for the Mini two years later.

1964 Paddy Hopkirk wins the Monte-Carlo Rally in a Mini-Cooper S. BMC launch the 1800 series and Mini Moke, and Issigonis is appointed as Engineering Director of BMC.

1965 Automatic version of the Mini available, but mechanical problems prevent quantity production until 1967.

1966 Mini-Coopers place first, second and third on the Monte-Carlo Rally, but are disqualified for a minor rule infringement.
Production Mini-Coopers fitted with twin fuel tanks.

1967 Mk2 Mini launched with larger rear lights, revised radiator grille and 998cc engine. Alec Issigonis appointed as a Fellow of the Royal Society.

1968 BMC becomes part of the British Leyland Motor Corporation Ltd. Production Minis fitted with 'wind-up' windows and door hinges mounted internally.

1969 Alec Issigonis honoured with a knighthood for his services to automotive engineering. Clubman version of the Mini introduced with revised nosecone designed by Roy Haynes.

1971 Production of the Mini-Cooper S ends, and Issigonis retires, but is retained on a consultancy basis for experimental vehicle work.

1974 1275GT Mini available with 'run-flat' Dunlop Denovo wheels and tyres, which could be safely used after a puncture at speeds of up to 50mph.

1975 The 1000 Special model, in a choice of Glacier White or Brooklands Green, marks the first of many limited edition models.

1982 Production of the Mini panelvan, estate and pick-up trucks is discontinued.

1984 The Mini's twenty fifth production anniversary is marked by the launch of the luxury Mini 25.

1988 Sir Alec Issigonis dies in Birmingham at the age of 81.

1989 ERA Mini Turbo fitted with a Garrett T3 turbocharger is debuted. Developing 96bhp at 6130rpm the car is good for 110mph.

1991 Modern version of the Mini-Cooper, and Mini Cabriolet are launched, both rejuvenating worldwide interest in the British classic.

1995 The Rover Group is sold to Munich-based car giant, BMW.

2000 BMW sell off their interests in Rover, but retain the right to produce the new Mini. Production of the traditional Mini ends after 41 years.

Today's Mini scene is bustling with greater activity and variety than at any time during the past as the number enthusiasts increases every year. Mini shows, and there are dozens throughout the year all over the world, attra thousands of people who share a common interest.

1

Making Minis

The first production Mini, made in 1959, was registered 621 AOK, painted white and is a treasured possession of the British Motor Industry Heritage Trust at Gaydon, Warwickshire. By comparison with modern machines, it is noisy, uncomfortable and crude, but completely wonderful to drive. Early cars suffered from rainwater leaks, but the handling and feeling of interior space are still marvels of design. AOK is pictured here with Paddy Hopkirk's famous 1964 Monte-Carlo Rally winner, also on display at Gaydon.

During the 1950s British car factories were thriving. Volkswagen's chief executive, Heinz Nordhoff, regarded British cars as the biggest threat to the dominant global position enjoyed by the Beetle at this time, and this threat inevitably increased after the BMC Mini's launch in 1959.

The car, which Leonard Lord ordered to be built to a brief that included economy, maximum interior space and low build costs, was born out of the 1956 Suez crisis. Issigonis made dozens of preliminary sketches for the bodywork, suspension and 948cc version of the BMC A series engine, which he had planned for transverse location.

At the same that BMW in Munich were heading in the direction of the bankruptcy courts – the Germany company's microcars, also borne out of the Suez crisis, had failed to save the German company's bacon – Issigonis and his small team were building Mini prototypes.

The development process was typically hurried and beset by niggling problems. In the summer of 1958 Leonard Lord drove a prototype for himself and, suitably impressed, ordered the car to be put into production.

Serious teething problems were twofold. The engine had been mounted with the carburettor and inlet manifold facing the front of the car, which led to carburettor icing and 'lumpy' running. This was solved by rotating the engine/gearbox unit through 180 degrees, so that the distributor, plugs and ignition leads faced the front – with predictable results in wet weather.

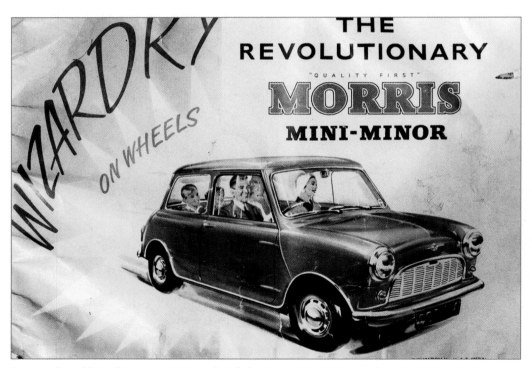

From early publicity literature, BMC marketed the Morris Mini-Minor and Austin Se7en (as they were officially badged), as 'Wizardry on Wheels', although the two words in small print – 'Quality First' – stretched credibility a little far in the early days of production. After surviving almost certain bankruptcy in 1959, BMW were working on a new saloon – the 1500 – at this time, which also had such severe quality problems that a senior member of the German company was moved to describe it as a 'shit car'.

FAR
MORE
ROOM
IN FAR
LESS
SPACE

This amazing Morris Mini-Minor engine is the product of one
of the greatest technical teams in the motor industry. Engine,
gears, and drive-axle, are all mounted in one brilliantly designed

Yet it is really the development of a tried and trusted friend; the

Apart from its low running costs and class-unrivalled roadholding, one of the Mini's strongest selling points was its deceptively large cabin. Issigonis had achieved this by placing the wheels at the extreme corners, fitting extremely narrow backrests to the diminutive seats, and by creating an extremely small boot at the rear. The transversely located engine and gearbox served to reduce overall length to give the kind of compactness that hadn't been seen in car design previously.

The second fright concerned engine performance. Although of diminutive capacity the 948cc 4-cylinder power unit, fed by a 1.25in SU carburettor, developed 37bhp which, with a trailing wind and downhill gradient, was sufficient to propel the prototype to a maximum speed of around 90mph. As the little car was aimed at drivers of all abilities, including those who select a gear for the day and use the rear-view mirror as a beauty-consultation aid, this was considered excessive.

As a result of fears expressed principally by test drivers, the cubic capacity was defined at 848cc from a bore and stroke of 62.9mm x 68.3mm. With a compression ratio of 8.1:1 and single SU HS2 carburettor, maximum power of 34bhp was developed at 5500rpm and there was 44lb/ft of torque at 2900rpm.

Top speed of 72mph was equal to that of the contemporary 30bhp 1200cc VW Beetle, and 60mph from rest was possible in around 34secs. Such figures are almost laughable today but in 1959 the highest speed achieved by the majority of ordinary British people was an extremely brisk trot between a church and the nearest pub.

One of the clever parts of the engineering packaging was the 4-speed gearbox, which was built into the engine's sump, and utilized engine oil for lubrication. Initially, this led to minor problems with seals blowing and oil fouling the clutch, but this proved to be relatively simple to remedy.

Suspension, jointly developed by Issigonis and Alec Moulton, was independent at all four corners but, instead of traditional springing media, there were rubber cones.

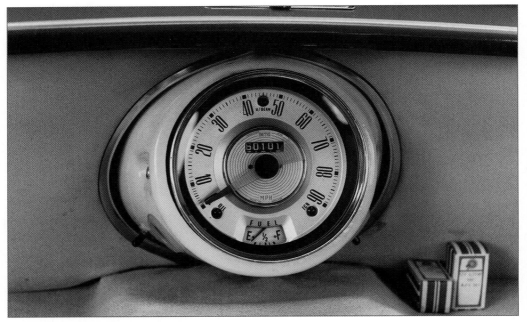

Economy of design included minimal instrumentation, the single speedometer and integral fuel gauge being prominently placed in the centre of the open facia. Europe's other great 'people's' cars – the Volkswagen Beetle, Citroën 2CV and Fiat 500 – also had minimal instrumentation (the Beetle was even without a fuel gauge until 1960), and for very good reason – other gauges were not necessary. The Mini's 'dashboard' shelf was extremely useful for storing odds and ends – a couple of light bulbs here – which usually rattled on to the floor under cornering.

Issigonis had experimented with this system before the Second World War with a single-seater racing car, the Lightweight Special, which he and George Dowson built entirely by hand. This Lightweight, incidentally, is campaigned today in hillclimb events by Dowson's son, Chris.

As applied to the Mini there were vertically mounted cones at the front, but those at the rear were mounted in the subframe, both arrangements performing a superb job in their intended role and having the additional advantage of light weight. Steering was by rack and pinion and gave almost kart-like precision in corners, and the 10in diameter steel road wheels, which indirectly helped to create such a roomy cabin, held surprisingly firm control on rough road surfaces.

In some respects the cabin's interior showed Issigonis's true design mastery, for although it was executed by production engineers to keep costs to a minimum, no other car of its size boasted as much usable space. In contemporary fashion the window glass area was commendably large, giving the interior a bright ambience and excellent all-round vision and, in Land-Rover style, the windows in the doors were of the sliding variety. The latter provision, along with concave doors and simple cords instead of door handles, was to maximise elbow room.

The useful oddments bins in both doors were inspired by the dairy industry, which, in Britain in the 1950s, sold milk in pint bottles. As an eminently practical chap, Issigonis had experienced the difficulty of finding a suitable place to safely carry a pint of milk by car, and the door bins provided a useful solution to a perennial problem.

Fashioned from hard black plastic the Mini's two-spoke steering wheel, with either the Morris or Austin symbol in the centre of the hub, was as uninspiring an object as most mass-produced items at the end of the 1950s. Owners with sporting aspirations – measured in hundreds of thousands by the mid-1960s – changed the standard wheel for a smaller, more 'racy' item.

Rubber mats on the floor area, vinyl-covered seats, minimal instrumentation placed in the centre of the open facia and a large diameter steering wheel positioned to give the familiar feeling of driving a miniature truck, early Minis were basic. What you saw is what you got. A push-button starter was mounted on the floor, a heater (considered to be 'namby-pamby' in some British motoring circles) was an extra-cost option and the boot, with its bottom-hinged lid, was capable of holding very little.

A de luxe version of the car had floor carpeting and two-tone vinyl seat covers but, despite the presence of the former, engine and gearbox noise was always intrusive, and fatiguing on long journeys. I once enjoyed the great privilege of driving Paddy Hopkirk's 1964 Monte-winning car, and seriously wondered how the great Irish driver had lived with his 'Min-bin' between London and the south-east coast, let alone as far as Prince Rainier's little country.

Two 'badge-engineered' cars – the Austin Seven (or Se7en in its earliest form) and the Morris Mini-Minor – were part of the original line-up. 'Mini' was a nickname, as was 'Beetle' for the Volkswagen saloon, but 'Mini' stuck, and for rather obvious reasons. It was a big car in miniature, and retailing at less than £600, an instant hit in Britain.

Apart from providing the masses with inexpensive transport that used fuel frugally, and was easy and cheap to maintain, the Mini quickly evolved into both a racing car and fashion accessory in a new decade of vast political, economic and social change. Like the Beetle, Fiat 500 and Citroën 2CV, the Mini was unique in its way, enjoyed an appeal beyond the boundaries of its mechanical specification and was entirely classless.

Although the Mini was hailed as being radical, and even revolutionary, by some, the car's radiator grille illustrated perfectly the conservative nature of the car-buying public. A chromed radiator grille had been a necessary, familiar and distinguishing

Opening rear side windows were something of a luxury. European manufacturers who made similar items usually offered them as expensive extra-cost options, as was the case with the Volkswagen Beetle. In the Mini they provided welcome fresh air, especially for parents with terminally travel-sick children.

feature of all conventional cars since pioneering days. The Mini's grille, however, was a piece of sheer nonsense.

Cold air for the water radiator, mounted 'north-south' on the left-hand side of the engine compartment, was ducted through slots in the left-hand inner wing. A front-mounted radiator grille was, therefore, unnecessary and from the point of view of protecting the distributor and plug leads from rainwater, the car would have been much improved without one. The grille, 'fake' that it was, did at least give the car a most delightful frontal appearance.

Added to the Mini range in 1960 were the estate versions with decorative wooden side trim. The choice was between the Morris-Mini Traveller and Austin Seven Countryman. 'Woodies' were hangovers from the days when cars were coachbuilt by hand, but not everyone warmed to the appearance of the Mini versions and, from 1962, these cars were optionally available without wood trim.

For the car-buying public the early 1960s was a most exciting period, as manufacturers in Britain and mainland Europe launched one advanced machine after another. After the sensation of the Mini's launch, Jaguar debuted the E-Type at the 1961 Geneva Motor Show. Just two years later Daimler-Benz launched the 230SL Pagoda, and Porsche exhibited the 901, or 911 as it was later known. Each of these cars broke new ground in some way or other. It was a most fertile time for automotive designers, who correctly took advantage of society's newly discovered affluence.

The Beatles, Rolling Stones, the Bay of Pigs fiasco (when the world came close to all-out nuclear war), Carnaby Street, 'Twiggy' (Lesley Hornby), the Peace and Hippie Movements, greater sexual freedom, man's first Moon landing and the BMC Mini all played important parts in shaping the 1960s, but the Mini's spirit has endured better than most icons of those hedonistic times.

Creeping comforts

Among the first steps towards a 'luxury' Mini was the production of two variants, the Wolseley Hornet and Riley Elf, which both debuted in October 1961. Neither of these cars was remotely connected with the two famous British car producers, which had become part of the British Motor Corporation in the early 1950s, but for some, the names gave these revised Minis something of an air of middle-class refinement.

Purely as 're-badging' and restyling exercises these cars were fair game for ridicule, but they held strong practical advantages over the standard Mini, the most useful of which was the extended boot at the rear with a top-hinged lid. There were revised taillamps, and the external body seams that featured on the Mini were absent from the hindquarters. Unlike the Mini, the Riley and Wolseley also had concealed, internal door hinges, which gave the flanks a neater and less workmanlike appearance. There were sturdier front and rear bumpers, and the radiator grille was wholly revised in the style of traditional 1950s Rileys and Wolseleys.

Chromed vertical grilles with horizontal side bars containing the indicators on their outer edges gave these cars a wholly different appearance. A Riley or Wolseley badge appeared in the centre of the grille, the latter being illuminated in time-honoured Wolseley fashion – a nice touch that made these cars instantly recognisable during the hours of darkness.

The interiors of these cars were either luxurious, or gimmicky, depending upon your point of view. Wind-up windows and door panelling negated the Mini's advantage of useful elbow room, but there was cloth upholstery, or leather at extra cost, and good quality carpeting adorned the floor panels. Seats in both variants were more generously padded than the standard Mini, and much more comfortable over long journeys.

In the Wolseley there was a piece of wood veneer applied to the oval instrument binnacle, while the Riley version received a 'full-width' dashboard, with gloveboxes and swivelling air-distribution vents on both sides, wholly in polished wood veneer. With the latter arrangement, the speedometer and two auxiliary instruments were no longer housed in an oval, but neatly sunk into the wood for improved aesthetic 'blending'. These cars were also treated to an ignition/starter switch in the centre of the dashboard.

Several Mini owners took an instant liking to the Riley Elf's polished dashboards, and fitted similar items to their own cars. Needless to say, specialist customizing companies had a field day with the Mini and, down many years, produced countless dozens of variations on the Mini theme.

Improved in some respects as the Hornets and Elfs undoubtedly were, they carried an inevitable weight penalty of nearly 100lb over the standard Mini, and handling response felt just a little duller by comparison. Top speed, at 72mph, was identical to the Mini's, but both the Elf and Hornet flogged up to 60mph from rest in 36secs – some 2secs slower than the Mini. To the vast majority of owners – more than 5500 of them between the beginning of production and the advent of the Mk2 version in 1963 – such pedestrian acceleration was of little importance. The diminutive cars were perceived as useful, economical shopping holdalls, and in this role they performed admirably.

From 1963, both the Elf and Hornet were fitted with the much more satisfactory 998cc 4-cylinder engine. This was a wholly revised unit with a bore and stroke of 64.6mmx76.2mm. Power was increased to 40bhp at 5250rpm, and torque went up

Technical Developments in the Motor Industry No. 6—

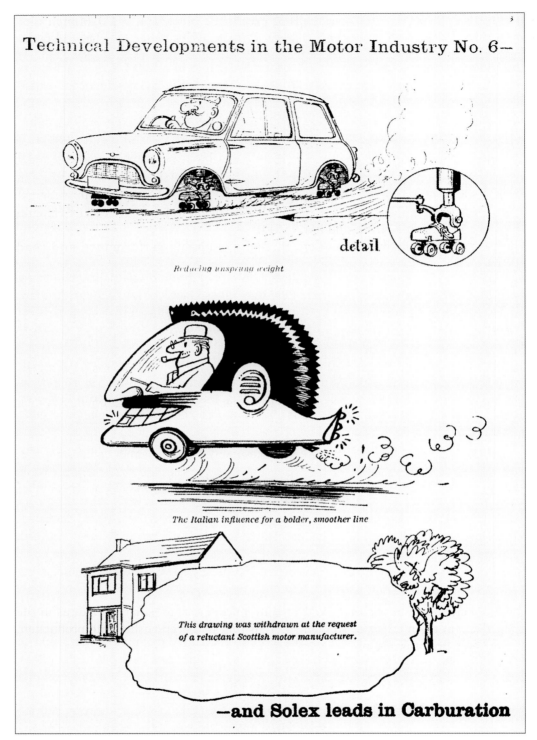

detail

Reducing unsprung weight

The Italian influence for a bolder, smoother line

This drawing was withdrawn at the request of a reluctant Scottish motor manufacturer.

—and Solex leads in Carburation

A stab at humour from *The Autocar*, January 1960, which sought to parody the Mini's small road wheels. Despite this light-hearted fun-poking the English publication, along with many other motoring journals, held the Mini's technical integrity in great esteem. Issigonis's engineering package inspired all, but it would take a further 15 years before Volkswagen and others would adopt the same technical layout for a new generation of passenger saloons.

to 52lb/ft at 2700rpm. Top speed was in excess of 80mph and the 0–60mph time tumbled to 27secs. All in all the car felt a lot more lively, better to drive and better balanced at speed, especially around corners. Thanks to wider brakes, anchor power was also superior.

Down the road

By 1963 the Mini was selling well, had gained an appreciable following and had clearly thrilled motor racing fans in national and club saloon car events in Britain. However, the small car market had become fiercely competitive and the choice had become ever wider. In roughly the same purchase price bracket as the Mini were the Renault 4, Citroen 2CV, Triumph Herald, Ford Anglia, Volkswagen Beetle, Hillman Imp, Fiat 500, Saab 2-stroke and BMW 700.

All of these cars were economical, had reasonable performance and road manners, despite the universal popularity of cross-ply tyres at this time, and were easy to maintain. BMC marketed the Mini under such slogans as: 'Far more room in far less space', 'Wizardry on wheels', and 'Big in performance! Big in comfort! Big in everything but cost and upkeep'.

By contemporary standards these claims were, by and large, absolutely spot-on, but the Mini had a lot more. Above all it provided driving enthusiasts with a cheap saloon that handled as well as, if not better than, a good few sports cars. Few drivers ever warmed to the quirky angle of the steering wheel, and tall folk found the driving position uncomfortable, but these were small niggles. One Mini owner known to this author, who stands at 6ft 7in, removed the driver's seat from his car and sat in the back!

The car's roadholding and handling broke new ground in small car design and, kept within sensible limits, it held on in corners in the manner of a teenager to its pocket money. With comparatively little horsepower, the normal front-wheel-drive vagaries – poor traction, torquesteer and understeer – were largely absent. After a number of Scandinavian rally drivers had demonstrated the technique of left-foot braking, it was shown that Minis could even be driven effectively in the manner of rear-drive cars.

'Everyday' Mini folk included the rich and famous. British film legend and car enthusiast, Peter Sellers, was among many who drove a Mini, Sellers's example having body flanks in wickerwork. The Mini quickly rose to 'smartcar' status in the 1960s but, in the manner of so many designs that had been rushed into production, it was not without problems.

Coughs and cures

Apart from the introduction of the Traveller and Countryman in September 1960, there was the Super version of the saloon from the autumn of 1961. This had conventional door handles, key-operated ignition, two-tone paint and circular oil and water temperature gauges to the right and left of the speedometer. The Mini name was adopted across the range from 1962, a move which pleased the dealer network.

In 1964, the famous hydrolastic suspension system was adopted for the Mini saloons, but early Mini developments primarily concerned the gearbox, which, although sound in design, had proved troublesome. Its weaknesses had come to light during the early days of competition, and during 1964 BMC's engineers produced a stronger but much simpler unit. Apart from strengthening the gear wheels and shafts, there was also a revised oil seal on the output shaft. Thereafter, the key to gearbox longevity lay in frequent oil and filter changes.

Despite these improvements, the quality of the gear change still left something to be desired. In 1965, during a rally organised by the once great Herefordshire Motor Club, my late father, mounted in the navigator's seat of a friend's Cooper S, shouted: 'Third gear, fast right over blind brow'. His driver heard the direction perfectly but fluffed third gear, and momentarily lost control of the car, which climbed a sycamore tree and gently fell backwards on to its roof. Dangling upside down the driver, who could hardly stop laughing, commented: 'I say, old boy, would you care for a banana – got a whole bunch of 'em in the boot!'

Encouraged by their remedial work on the manual gearbox, BMC began the precarious route towards the manufacture of a 4-speed automatic in 1965. The debut of the Mini automatic was, however, premature. The 'box' worked well when it worked at all, but initial problems with oil surge in corners showed lubricant starvation to the torque converter. A larger oil filter, relocation of the oil pump to the centre of the sump and increased oil capacity solved the problem.

Like so many of the best ideas, the Mini's ingenious layout is simple, but never to be under-estimated. With the 'east–west' location of the power unit, the radiator was cooled by air ducted through slots in the left-hand inner wing. Other than allowing rainwater in to dampen the electrical system, the function of the radiator grille was purely for decoration. Note the sturdy chassis crossmember under the seat.

The original 848cc in-line 4-cylinder engine developed a most healthy 37bhp, and allowed for a respectable maximum speed of 72mph. By comparison, Volkswagen's contemporary Beetle had a 1200cc engine developing 34bhp, which was also good enough for a top speed of 72mph. From rest the Mini could achieve the benchmark 60mph figure in around 38secs, comparable with figures achieved by peers from Saab, NSU, Volkswagen and Ford, et al.

The inherent, power-sapping nature of automatics led to a 9:1 compression ratio and revised SU carburettor, and power output from the 848cc engine consequently rose to 39.5bhp at 5250rpm, which compared favourably with the 40bhp developed by the contemporary 1.3-litre VW Beetle introduced in August 1965.

In many respects the mid-1960s was a happy time for the Mini. Scathing criticism from journalists was almost entirely absent from the most influential specialist journals, and Japanese manufacturers had yet to gain a foothold in Western markets. Despite the happy absence of these thorns, though, BMC were not in especially good shape.

The company had a plethora of models that, for a variety of reasons, were expensive to make. Pruning and rationalisation were needed – fewer 'one-make' floorpans, for example, would have provided both a long- and short-term solution to the hefty cost of production – but Corporation boss Lord Stokes battled on largely in ignorance of the stark realities of modern-day economics.

However, four victories in a row on the Monte-Carlo Rally between 1964 and 1967 – three wins if the 1966 farce is excluded – had brought unprecedented publicity for the little car, and in Britain particularly, it seemed that almost everyone wanted to own and drive a Mini.

In 1967, BMC launched the Mk2 version and at the same time appointed senior stylist Roy Haynes to the board of directors.

Cleverly built into the engine's sump, and lubricated by engine oil, early gearboxes were not among the Mini's strong points. After a spate of blown oil seals, BMC made modifications, and went as far as substantially strengthening the gear wheels in 1964. Gearchanging itself was never a particularly slick or smooth operation – more akin to opening a semi-collapsed Radnorshire farm gate – but was, nevertheless, part of the Mini's innate charm and character.

Designed by Alex Moulton, the suspension was not by traditional coil or torsion-bar springing, but rubber cones built into the subframes. This was changed in 1964 for the largely unloved hydrolastic system, which tended to give a more 'choppy' ride, and less sure-footed roadholding characteristics. Moulton's rubber suspension was later used on a bicycle – the Mini Moulton – a modern version of which remains popular among well-heeled cyclists today.

A beautifully preserved early Austin version of the Mini sits among many other prize exhibits at Gaydon. By 1960, those who had cottoned on to the car's finer points, and the many advantages it held over traditional wallowing ~ons from some parts of the British car industry, queued at dealers' showrooms in increasing numbers. The ~gest problem the car held for the British Motor Corporation was that it only rarely showed a profit.

~ether it made a profit for BMC or not, the Mini was ~E car that turned its back on the 1950s, and became ~ automotive icon of the 1960s and beyond. Like the ~ndful of other people's cars, the Mini was 'classless', ~d appealed to all. In some quarters it became a fashion ~essory.

Popularly dubbed the 'Tudor Cottage' by journalists, the estate version, with decorative wooden trim á là Mor
Minor Traveller, was based on the panelvan. The two versions, Morris Mini-Traveller and Austin Sev
Countryman, had double rear doors and gave an appreciable gain in luggage space over the standard salo
British manufacturers were among the few who continued to use wood in car construction during the 1960s.

One of the most useful utility vehicles ever made, the Mini van was an early addition to the range, and ser
tradesfolk well for several decades. As a light delivery vehicle it had few rivals and, like its saloon counterpart, v
endowed with excellent fuel consumption. Like Volkswagen's classic Transporter panelvan, Mini vans led su
hard lives that relatively few survive in good condition.

Mercedes' Clean Sweep

1st, 2nd, 3rd IN THE 29th MONTE CARLO RALLY: SUNBEAM RAPIER BEST-PLACED BRITISH FINISHER

In conditions typical of most of the routes in this year's Monte Carlo Rally, the Morley brothers' Mini-Minor chases the Sunbeam Rapier driven by Stephens and Corbett towards the Col de la Machine, during the Mountain Circuit

CHALLENGING the theory, so often demonstrated during the past two years, that the most suitable car for a rally is a small, high-performance saloon, three large and comfortable, factory-sponsored Mercedes-Benz 220SE saloons have swept the board in the Monte Carlo Rally, taking first three places in the general classification, and the team prize. Throughout the event, they were impressively well-driven in the icy conditions, and despite many, many miles of high-speed motoring along narrow Alpine roads, they were unscratched at the finish. It was said that the successful cars, together with drivers and mechanics, had been at Monte Carlo for three months before the event, practising until the crews knew the all-important Mountain Circuit inside out. This demonstrates, once and for all, that—provided one has sufficient time and money to spare—rallying need not be the lottery that so many people think it is.

Highest-placed British car was again a Sunbeam Rapier, driven by Peter Harper and Raymond Baxter, which finished in fourth position. Through extremely bad fortune, they had lost nine minutes (90 penalty marks) on the road section; however, without these they would still have failed to make third position. Fifth place went also to a Mercedes-Benz 220SE, and all these four Mercedes had started from Warsaw. A privately-entered Ford Zephyr, driven by Sutcliffe and Crabtree, took sixth position—in fact beating the three factory-entered Zephyrs which at one time had looked like doing so well.

The winners, Schock and Moll, wait in their Mercedes-Benz 220SE while the marshal records their arrival at a passage control

PROVISIONAL GENERAL CLASSIFICATION

1 Mercedes-Benz 220SE (Schock and Moll, Germany).
2 Mercedes-Benz 220SE (Bohringer and Socher, Germany).
3 Mercedes-Benz 220SE (Ott and Mahle, Germany).
4 Sunbeam Rapier (Harper and Baxter, Britain).
5 Mercedes-Benz 220SE (Tak and Swaab, Germany).
Coupe des Dames: Austin A 40 (Pat Moss and Ann Wisdom, Britain).
Team Prizes: 1, Mercedes-Benz. 2, DKW. 3, Ford.

The factory entered 848cc Minis for several high-profile rally events from 1959 to 1961, but although underpowered, they handled well and were endowed with good traction on loose surfaces. This clipping from *The Autocar* shows that Mercedes-Benz were all-conquering on the 1960 Monte, but early Mini successes included sixth overall for David Seigle-Morris on the 1960 RAC Rally, and a class win for Peter Riley on the 1961 Tulip Rally.

A late model Mini pick-up truck captured at a *concours d'elegance* in 2000. Fitted with smart 'Minilite' al
wheels, wheelarch extensions and spotlamps, this personalised vehicle gets away from the utility nature of
original concept – the Mini pick-up was also launched in 1960 – but, as this picture clearly illustrates, little of
basic idea was changed in 30 years.

Endowed with all of the saloon's many attributes, the pick-up was a familiar sight on British roads for more th
three decades. It was a firm favourite among farmers, builders, plumbers and similar trades and, according
many, should never have been killed off. In Britain today, the pick-up market is heavily dominated by Japan
manufacturers, a situation for which British car makers have only themselves to blame.

The pick-up's tailgate was bottom-hinged and supported on metal stays, but one particularly clever design touch was that of the number plate, which automatically dropped into a vertical position when the tailgate was lowered. The owner of this vehicle has fitted wood panelling to the bed, sides, wheel arches and tailgate to protect the bodywork, but this wasn't a standard arrangement.

Another absolutely lovely 'period' piece from *The Autocar*, March 1961, featuring a high-quality sunroof from the Knighton Motor Trimming Company of Surrey. Made of high-quality PVC, the sunroof cost £21 15s, and an extra £2 10s for a lockable version. The Mini lent itself particularly well to 'add-ons', and for many years, accessory suppliers made handsome capital – unlike the Mini's manufacturer.

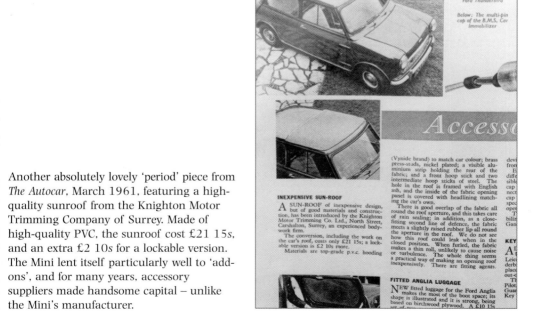

By the spring of 1960 the Mini had made such a huge impact on British motoring life, that it was used as a cover picture for *The Autocar* in March 1961, despite a road test in the same issue on the brand new, and highly acclaimed, Jaguar E-Type. In many respects, both cars were huge British success stories, and the products of an exciting new decade, but everything turned pear-shaped under the leaky shelter of the British Leyland umbrella.

In January 1962 the Issigonis 'miracle' car was officially known as the Mini. The Austin Seven and Morris Mini-Minor names were discarded, because they were a mouthful and the car had become known, virtually everywhere, as the Mini. Austin and Morris badging, however, was kept, the two cars being identifiable externally by a slight difference in the design of the radiator grilles.

Owned by English enthusiast Don Gregory, this immaculate 1962 car was found in a garage, where it had languished from 1967 to 1991. When Don discovered it the car had covered just 17,000 miles. Over a period of four years he restored it bodily and mechanically – it had rusted in all the 'usual' Mini places – and it is now driven on a regular basis. Apart from a faulty fuel pump which needed replacing, the car is completely reliable.

The 'cooking' 848cc engine in Don Gregory's car was rebuilt to exactly the correct and original specification. There are few simpler power units and, in contrast to modern engines, everything is easily accessible for servicing and maintenance. Thankfully, parts for Minis are plentiful, readily available and many are extremely cheap to buy. Often recommended as an 'ideal first car', many folks never grow out of Minis and understandably so.

Although in some ways resembling the turret of a modern MacPherson strut, and unfamiliar to the owners of many early Minis, this item to the right of the engine block, left of the picture, is the optional blower/heater. Even as late as the early 1960s, the presence of a heater could not be taken for granted, but was a welcome addition, particularly during the extremely cold and long British winter of 1963.

de luxe version of the Mini with conventional door handles and floor carpeting featured from the early days of production. The speedometer on this late 1962 example is also flanked by a temperature gauge, left, and oil pressure gauge, right. Of these additions, floor carpeting was arguably the most useful, as its most valuable contribution was in damping down noise from the engine and gearbox.

In October 1961, BMC launched two variations on the Mini theme in the form of the Riley Elf (illustrated) and Wolseley Hornet. Both cars were 'badge-engineered', luxury versions of the standard Mini saloon, the most obvious differences being the traditional radiator shells and extended boot at the rear for additional luggage-carrying capacity.

The frontal styling was wholly in keeping with traditional Riley aesthetics, the shape of the chromed radiator grille, blue badge and decorative horizontal slats largely maintaining the spirit of a once great, but defunct, British marque. The 'Mini with a boot' also differed from the standard model in having attractive swage lines and a chromed strip on the bonnet, and rectangular indicator lenses.

Boot badging was in a traditional script, and gave the Elf and Hornet a distinctive 'up-market' image, that in one respect recognized the emergence of a segregated, and unmistakeably English, middle class. During 1961 and 1969 (when production ended) Rileys slightly outsold the Wolseley versions, but neither model was a huge success in terms of volume numbers.

The interior of the Riley Elf retained the Mini's 'upright' steering column and large-diameter steering wheel and the facia was in highly polished wood veneer – a traditional touch at which English manufacturers excelled. Leather seats (illustrated) were available at extra cost, and added greatly to the cabin's ambience of hand-crafted, Bentley-like luxury. Note that a glovebox was fitted on both sides of the dashboard.

Because Elfs and Hornets were heavier than Minis, they were also underpowered with the original 848cc engine, 2secs slower than the Mini from 0–60mph. In 1963 both 'booted' variants were fitted with the 998cc 40t engine, which increased top speed to 80mph, and brought the 0–60mph time tumbling to 27secs. Su performance in a small saloon was distinctly 'sizzling' by the standards of the day and, coupled with wid acclaimed roadholding properties, there was little in its class to touch it.

Externally, Wolseley Hornets were almost identical to Elfs – the Mk3 version opposite is without externally-mounted door hinges – wit the obvious exception of the badge mounted o the radiator grille which, in true Wolseley tradition, was illuminated when the lights wer switched on. Small but important details like t gave cars of the 1950s and 1960s an individu and instantly recognisable identity . . .

. . . which became completely lost during the 1970s and 1980s: just one reason for the success of the classic car movement and the birth of many old-car magazines whose contributors continued to extol the virtues of traditional car design.

Garage proprietor, Angelo Barbierato, continues to use his unrestored 1967 Hornet everyday transport. Well-known in Mini circles, Angel has never believed in pampering his steed, and considers the Wolseley to be among the most 'fun' cars ever made. Fitted with alloy wheels, and devoid of bumpers, his example has th sporting appearance of a Cooper S and travel-scarred gait of a hill farmer caught i a nasty blizzard.

Less expensive to buy than the Riley, the Hornet's dashboard, although more plush than the standard Mini's, had wood veneer confined to an 'oval' surrounding the three gauges. This gave a hint of traditional craftsmanship, but left the advantage of the standard open facia-cum-parcel shelf which, unlike the Riley's gloveboxes, gave ready access for bits and bobs.

After the production of approximately 31,000 Riley Elfs, and 29,000 Wolseley Hornets, the car-buying pub finally saw the back of these cars in 1969 under the directorship of British Leyland. At this juncture, th huge company was in desperate need of rationalisation, especially as the many bad days of the 1970s were just around the corner. Loyal customers mourned the passing of the and Hornet but, by way of consolation, the Mini remained as popular as ever.

iginally intended as a light military vehicle, but launched in 1964 for civilian use, the Mini Moke achieved lt' status, despite UK production ending in 1968 after 14,518 examples had been completed. The vast majority re exported to warmer climes. Production was continued in Australia, and in Portugal from 1984, and the ɔke remains as popular everyday transport in several Mediterranean countries.

' the cars built in Britain between 1964 and 1968, fewer than 1,500 were sold on the home market, where the t-inclement weather did not lend itself especially well to a car with a rudimentary soft-top, and an excess of ɔow room owing to the total lack of doors. Mokes made in Portugal from 1991 had improved weather otection, 12in diameter road wheels, galvanised bodywork and a lockable luggage compartment.

Based wholly on the Mini's mechanicals, and fitted with rubber-cone suspension, the Moke had similar road characteristics to its saloon counterpart. With such rudimentary weather protection, though, the Moke, above 45mph, always felt a little like landing a microlight in a field of terrified sheep. I once accomplished this and found it to be bumpy, loo-beckoning and never to be repeated. The sheep probably felt the same way.

The Swinging Sixties recreated at the British Motor Industry Heritage Trust, Gaydon in the Nervous Nineties. Minis, Mokes, mini-skirts and other radical fashions were all part of a 'pop' decade of huge social, economic and political upheaval. The Beatles, Rolling Stones and Beach Boys regularly topped the charts, the world's two 'super powers' viewed each other coldly through the sights of nuclear weapons, and the Peace Movement emerged to offer a powerful message to western governments, that war was not a satisfactory answer to solving political disputes. Forty years on, mistakes of the past continue to be repeated.

...er the debut of the 997cc twin-carburettor Mini-
...per on the 1962 Monte-Carlo Rally – Stirling Moss's
...er, Pat, collected the ladies' prize in 737 ABL on this
...nt – the Mini's reputation as a sound competition car
...an to grow. The works cars on this event developed
...und 85bhp which, in a car weighing around half
...t of a traditional rally machine, gave the late John
...per huge potential for development.

...ind the scenes at BMC during the mid-1960s, the designers were working on a number of different projects
...uding this MG-based two-seater sports car. With body styling by Pininfarina it was, like the Mini, fitted with
...n diameter wheels and had front-wheel drive, but it got no further than prototype stage. Although
...eptionally pleasant to drive, it is doubtful if production cars would have seriously challenged sales of the
...rting contemporary Austin-Healey Sprites and MG Midgets.

Meanwhile, *The Autocar*, and other journals, were so enthusiastic about 'Mini Magic', that the car continued to be featured in pride of place on the cover well into the 1960s. As the cover line makes clear, the Mini was 'setting the pace in performance, and beating traffic'. This was certainly true on British roads, but exports were thin at first. For all British and European manufacturers North America had the greatest potential for exports, but the Mini was never to succeed in a country that clearly had no need of a small, economical 'runabout'.

At the same that the Pininfarina-bodied sports car was being mooted, Mini enthusiasts had their own sports car – the Cooper S – and, unlike the MG-based prototype on the previous page, the Mini had the distinct advantage of four seats. Largely thanks to the publicity that ensued from two successive victories on the Monte-Carlo Rally by 1965, the Mini had become Britain's best-loved car at this time.

One of many Mini rivals during the 1960s, the 600cc rear-engined NSU Prinz (pronounced 'Prints') was endowed with a 0–50mph potential of 17.9secs, and good handling, but it failed to capture a large slice of the British market. Potential customers for small cars rarely took to the NSU's bath tub styling, and even fewer warmed to the idea of an air-cooled engine in the rear.

The Mini-Coopers entered for the 1962 Monte were fitted with front disc brakes, which held huge benefits over traditional drums. Discs had been developed by Dunlop, and used to great effect by Jaguar at Le Mans in the 1950s. By 1963, when this advertisement for Girling discs appeared in *The Autocar*, the Porsche 356 and newly-launched Mercedes-Benz 230SL had disc brakes but, generally, this was an area of automotive design in which Germany fell some way short of Britain.

During the early 1960s Austin developed their industrial turbine engine. Developing 250 shaft horse power, and working at a speed of 29,000rpm, it was intended for industrial applications, and as a road car power unit. Rover had been working on similar units for many years – the Rover BRM sports car ran successfully at Le Mans – but gas turbine engines were subsequently discovered to be unsuited to road application.

nparatively low engine power, and the excellent traction afforded by the weight of the engine and transmission
·ctly over the driving wheels, endowed the Mini with all-terrain grip. Captured here on a rough road in Africa,
; vast continent didn't particularly embrace the Mini, as the largely unmade roads were more suitable for the
id Rover, which became a best-seller in virtually every African country.

By October 1967 the Mini, which had been in production for eight years, was treated to a minor facelift a relaunched as the Mk2. The changes were of a relatively minor nature, except that the 998cc engine beca available in the 'cooking' car, and performance was greatly improved over the original 848cc unit. During dying years of the 1960s, all manufacturers were forced by legislation to make cars safer, and exhaust emissi cleaner. As a result of these changes great British classics, like the Austin-Healey 3000, fell by the wayside, w the Mini marched forward – as usual.

2

The Mini growing up

The Mk1's rear lights were rounded, small and elegant, but inconspicuous. By the mid-1960s traffic growth in Britain and Europe was such that much larger lights were required.

In October 1967 BMC launched the Mk2 version of the Mini, which was greeted with rapturous applause. While the German economy had dipped uncharacteristically into recession in the mid-1960s, Britain was booming by comparison and there was a tangible sense of optimism. The memory of England winning the 1966 World Cup final against Germany was still fresh in British minds, although the Torrey Canyon oil disaster – the first of many supertanker catastrophes – of the following year dampened spirits a little and brought a new word – 'environment' – into the vocabulary of everyday folk.

Car safety, principally inspired by American lawyer Ralph Nader, had become a hotly debated public issue. Because of Nader's efforts car manufacturers who exported their products to North America were forced to mend their ways or seek export markets elsewhere. Nader's ideas were enshrined in US legislation – from 1967 the reduction of harmful exhaust emissions had also become an important issue in the design of engines – and manufacturers had little option but to comply.

As North America was not among the Mini's important export markets, it soldiered on in Mk2 form as a 'facelifted' but actually improved car. By 1967, of course, it had been in production for eight years, or roughly the same period in which modern cars are kept in production before being replaced. There was, however, little need to change the Mini's fundamental design because it was bang-on 'out of the bag'.

For those who didn't warm to the Mini's finer points, BMC made the larger 1100 and 1300 saloons as alternatives, but these aesthetically dreary lemons were among the dullards of the British motor industry, and served to increase both the magic, and the cult following enjoyed by Issigonis's masterwork.

The Mk2 Mini retained its sliding windows, external door hinges and chrome trim – Lamborghini pioneered the use of matt black trim on the Miura, also launched in 1967 – but the most obvious exterior changes were to the tail lamps and radiator grille. The former were larger, rectangular and, in the opinion of many, much more attractive. A broad band of chrome was applied to the perimeter of the radiator grille, which also had angled bottom left- and right-hand corners. To distinguish between Austin and Morris versions, the former had horizontal grille bars, while the Morris got vertically positioned ones.

Interestingly, the chromed bar along the leading edge of the bonnet, which formed the top piece to the radiator grille, failed on many examples to align itself with the rest of the trim, and gave additional firepower to critics, who were beginning to suspect that BMC build quality was wanting. Mini enthusiasts dismissed this quirk as being part of the car's charm and innately unique character that enhanced its image as a fun car.

One piece of this character, however, disappeared for good in the middle of 1968 when the crude 'string' door-pulls were replaced by conventional door handles. This change was brought about by growing affluence, but is a typical example of how cars put on weight unnecessarily as they are developed. Simple cords to operate the door catches, incidentally, made a reappearance in 1972 – not on a crudely appointed people's car, but on the Porsche Carrera 911 RS Lightweight!

Although the 848cc Mini remained as the staple of the range, a 998cc version was available from 1967 and inevitably fitted to the Mk2 saloon and estate bodies. Sharing the same 64.6mm x 76.2mm bore and stroke as the earlier Elfs, Hornets

One of the most obvious changes to the Mk2 version of the Mini, launched in October 1967, was the slight but distinctive alteration in the shape of the chromed radiator grille. The top three grilles in this illustration are the rounded Mk1 units, while the later grilles – the bottom three – had 'squared-off' side pieces. Like most parts for the Mini, replacement grilles are readily available.

Similar to the treatment Volkswagen brought to the Beetle at the same time, the Mk2 Mini's rear lights were made much larger and, in contrast to the curves of the bodywork, were rectangular. These lamps slightly altered the car's aesthetics – the Mini adopted a much more modern look – and many argued that they were a great improvement.

and Coopers, the Mini 1000, as it was dubbed, developed 38bhp at 5250rpm. With a compression ratio of 8.3:1 and a single SU HS2 carburettor, the car was capable of 0–60mph in 22secs and a top speed of 75mph. An automatic gearbox was offered as an extra-cost option. First gear in manual gearboxes joined the top three ratios in also having synchromesh from 1968.

By 1969 the motoring world had taken a huge shift away from austerity, a move dictated naturally by growing affluence in the developed world. In this same year the Mini had been in production for 10 years, but its international rally career had been brought to an end by Porsche's 911 and Ford's all-conquering Escort. The Mini had been the 'wonder car' of the 1960s but, despite the age of the design, it remained as popular as ever, particularly in Britain.

The mini 'Ford'

As a small, spacious, compact car it was difficult to improve the fundamentally sound facets of the design – Issigonis really had got it right first time around – but simply because it had been in production for a long time, chief stylist Roy Haynes redesigned the Mini's nose and the Clubman version appeared for the first time in 1969.

Haynes's restyling exercise was controversial. Dyed-in-the-wool Mini enthusiasts never accepted the Clubman as an aesthetic improvement over the traditional Mini, while others considered it as an inevitable 'facelift' and warmed to it quickly. For the Clubman, Haynes retained circular headlamps, but placed them in a 'full-width' grille with horizontal chromed bars and a distinctive, vertical Clubman badge in the centre. The chromed bumper sat immediately below the grille, and the indicators were located below the bumper.

Classic circular headlamps and tiny indicator lenses – similar to those fitted to Land Rovers – remained to the same design as previously and, in the case of the headlamps, helped to create the illusion of a car with a human face. The VW Beetle was similarly endowed with the frontal appearance of a 'face', which is just one reason for these people's cars becoming so popular.

There was nothing especially radical or unconventional about the new design but, that it bore more than a passing resemblance to the Ford Cortina Mk2 was not a coincidence. Before joining BMC in 1967 Haynes had designed the Mk2 Cortina while working for Ford. Many regard this version of the Cortina as his magnum opus, for it finally kicked into touch the old Ford philosophy of building cars with Detroit-style 'fins-and-whistles'.

Haynes recognised Ford's British customers as conservative, and designed the Cortina as a bland, three-box saloon with a spacious cabin and rear luggage space – an ideal family hack. It was an instant hit, immensely profitable for Ford and justifiably gave Roy Haynes a degree of confidence in his future role as BMC's chief stylist.

Apart from the Mini Clubman, Haynes was also responsible for the Morris Marina – BMC's answer to the Ford Cortina Mk2. To the same three-box format with the engine mounted up front driving the rear wheels, the Marina also had a radiator grille that resembled those of the Mini Clubman and Cortina. However, the background to the Marina is illustrative of the pickle for which the company would become famous. Initially, Haynes' design for the Marina resembled a Jaguar. This was a reasonable starting point because, as Roy pointed out to this author, it doesn't cost any more money to make a family saloon that looks like a Jaguar than it does to produce an automotive dullard.

Upon viewing Haynes's initial drawings Lord Stokes warned Haynes to 'keep his nose out of Jaguar's affairs, and mind his own bloody business'. What became of the Marina project is well known! Haynes left BMC at the end of the 1960s to pursue a

The 998cc 4-cylinder engine was to the same basic design as the 848cc unit and, with a compression ratio of 8.3:1, developed 38bhp. This was good enough for a top speed of around 75mph, and a reasonable 0–60mph best of 22secs. One of the great advantages of all Mini power units has always been their relative simplicity. A skilled person can rebuild one to perfection in a matter of hours, and for very little financial outlay.

successful career as a freelance designer, leaving what would become British Leyland to contend with the vagaries of the 1970s.

However, among the Maxis, Marinas, Ambassadors and Allegros et al, the Mini remained supreme in the British small-car market. Despite its controversial looks the Haynes-designed Clubman was an extremely competent, able little car. And for those who couldn't warm to the revised nose, the interior provided ample compensation. In place of the 'basic' Mini's central instrument cluster, and minimalist approach to interior design, there was a much more conventional dashboard.

The top bar of the dashboard was padded and a three-spoke steering wheel replaced the traditional two-spoker. Instrumentation comprised a circular speedometer and combination fuel/water temperature gauge, which were housed in a black plastic binnacle directly in line with the driver. No longer was it necessary to peer at the gauges in the centre of the car to gain information about the various functions. Fresh-air ventilation was also improved by new vents at each end of the dashboard.

The growing club

In addition to the 'cooking' 1000cc Clubman, there was the 1275GT, introduced at the same time as its less 'sizzling' sister, and intended ultimately to replace the much-loved Cooper S (of which more anon). As its model designation indicates, the 1275GT was fitted with a 1275cc version of the in-line 4-cylinder engine with a bore and stroke of 70.6mm x 81.3mm and 8.8:1 compression ratio. Initially, power output was rated at 60bhp at 5250rpm, and maximum torque of 69.5lb/ft at 2500rpm.

Hydrolastic suspension was standard wear, although this was phased out in 1971 – across the entire range – and cheaper, but equally effective, rubber cones were fitted instead. Standard anchor power comprised discs up front and drums at the rear. Weighing slightly more than 1500lbs, the 1275GT wasn't the lightweight it might have been, and critics were apt to criticise its lacklustre performance which wasn't on a par with the Cooper S. This aside, the 1275GT was easily capable of a top speed of 87mph, and accelerating from standstill to 60mph in 13.5secs, figures which few contemporaries in the 'cooking' 1.3-litre class could match.

With its long-nose Clubman front end, the 1275GT was never as pretty as the Cooper S, and never accepted as a 'real' replacement for its illustrious predecessor, but had the normal Mini attributes that brought it acclaim from dozens of converts. Externally the car was distinguished by a set of attractive Rostyle steel wheels (shod with radial tyres), a 'go-faster' stripe along the lower flanks and Mini 1275GT badging at the bottom of the doors.

After the demise of the Cooper S in the summer of 1971, the 1275GT became the flagship of the Mini range, but there were dark days ahead for much of the motoring world. In 1972, for example, BMW planned to launch their new 5-series saloon to coincide with the Munich Olympic Games. This great sporting event, however, was marred by terrorist activity resulting in the tragic deaths of several Israeli athletes. Naturally, no-one took any notice of the new BMW.

The revised Clubman version of the Mini first appeared in 1969. This restyling exercise was penned by Roy Haynes, who joined the company board in 1967 from Ford. Roy had previously been responsible for the styling of the Mk2 Cortina which, as this illustration clearly shows, bore a resemblance to the Mini Clubman. Naturally, the revised styling had its devotees, but wasn't wholeheartedly embraced by Mini enthusiasts. Note the British Leyland badge in the centre of the grille of this late 1970s example.

After the rallying success of Minis during the 1960s, nearly all 'boy racers' invested in a mesh guard for the headlamps. This was not principally to protect the glassware, but as a stylish means of identifying more closely with motor sport. Mesh guards like these date back to the vintage days of the 1930s, when Bentleys, *et al.*, thundered around the dusty, rock-strewn roads of Le Mans.

The following year was marked by the politically engineered oil crisis in the Middle East, which led to fuel rationing in several European countries including Britain. For a short period it appeared that exotic gas-guzzling supercars had had their day, and economical cars like the Mini would come to the fore, but political turmoil on the international stage seemed trifling by comparison with the problems facing the board of British Leyland. Strikes became part and parcel of everyday life throughout much of British manufacturing industry by the mid-1970s, and the car industry suffered. Stand-up comedians made jokes about Skodas and Ladas, but it quickly became apparent that their efforts had been guided in the wrong direction. The world's really bad cars were manufactured closer to home.

It was a tragic era in British motor manufacturing history and a pitiful waste, because, behind the scenes, British engineers were hard at work as usual making improvements to their designs. One particularly clever innovation was the Dunlop Denovo tyre and wheel. These were fitted to the 1275GT in late 1974 – standard wear just three years later – and designed to run safely at speeds of up to 50mph, for a distance of 40 miles, in the event of a puncture. This was the first tyre of its kind fitted commercially to any vehicle.

Dunlop's tyre designer, Tom Holmes, was closely associated with this exciting project, but the innovative Denovo wasn't the first 'run-flat' tyre that had been fitted to the Mini. In the summer of 2000, Tom told me that several prototype Minis had been experimentally fitted with the 'run-flats' during 1958.

'They worked well enough,' he commented, 'and had the advantage that they were only 1in wide. This meant that the spare wheel took up very little space, and left additional luggage room that you didn't get with a tyre and rim of conventional size. Unfortunately, the design didn't go into production, because Dunlop were afraid that there would be too many production problems. For example, after a loss of air in these early 'run-flats', you couldn't repair them.

This was not the case with the Denovo, though. For its launch Dunlop invited the world's press to the Paul Ricard racing circuit in France. As a result of the ensuing publicity, Dunlop's shares rallied. 'We sold some 250,000 units in all, but they never really caught on.'

Unfortunately, they were expensive to buy, and the flexible walls of the tyres, which were 1cm thick, gave unfamiliar handling characteristics but, as a piece of innovation, this was another first for Britain.

From 1975 the 1275GT had reclining seats, and British Leyland also launched the first of many limited edition Minis, dubbed the Special. Finished in either green or white with a body 'coachline', these cars also had reclining front seats and there was an increase in engine power – up to 40bhp – clearly aimed at breathing new life into a car whose appeal was clearly flagging.

In the same year the standard Clubman's engine was increased in capacity to 1098cc. With a bore and stroke of 64.6mm x 83.7mm and a compression ratio of 8.5:1, the new unit produced a maximum of 45bhp at 5250rpm. Top speed rose to 84mph and standstill to 60mph could be attained in a whisker or two under 18secs but, despite the increase in performance, fuel consumption remained as monotonously impressive as ever.

By 1980, the Clubman range, including the 1275GT, was at an end. The last of the 1275GTs were distinguished with external matt black trim in keeping with contemporary motor industry trends, but the long-nosed car was finally axed to make way for the Metro.

In a production career spanning some 10 years, more than half a million Clubmans were sold, but Mini purists never accepted Roy Haynes' frontal styling. While the traditional Mini continued in production, British Leyland's hopes for the future in small-car manufacturing were pinned on the Metro. At the new car's public launch in 1980, British Leyland's chief executive Michael Edwardes secured the services of the plain-speaking Australian Grand Prix driver Alan Jones. In his customary manner, Jones publicly declared the Metro to be 'a bloody good little car'. It was not!

As the Metro had the convenience of a hatchback body, the traditional Mini estate car would also be axed from the range in 1982, which many enthusiasts regarded as a backward step. The Metro sold steadily but although possessed of the Mini's many virtues – good fuel economy, excellent cabin space and lively performance – it had none of the hallmarks of a classic. Many considered the styling to be unsatisfactory and, given the company's history, it was almost inevitable that build-quality problems would rear their ugly heads.

Body rust became a perennial curse of the Metro, but more serious was the media publicity given to the early cars' occasional propensity for leaking petrol from the fuel filler neck on to a rear tyre. This problem was corrected but added fuel to the fire of the many critics who had given up on British Leyland, or as many remarked: 'Whatever it calls itself these days'.

An endorsement of the Mini's reliability and sheer practical value, many of Britain's police forces adopted Minis as 'Panda' cars during the 1960s and 1970s. As a hot motorway pursuit vehicle aimed at catching the Hon. J. Bonnington-Jagsworth in his speeding E-Type, the Mini was next-to-useless but, as a local plodder, it was excellent for transporting yobs from Saturday night watering holes to Dock Green for a night in a darkened room.

speed, brute strength...
perfect response
ore than a mile a minute

Goodyear's radial tyre that
AL DRIVING CONTROL:
ive block tread grips
lds steady and sure in
TAL TYRE TOUGHNESS:
ar's exclusive Tracsyn
rd construction.
E : Over double the mileage
est-selling conventional
PERFORMANCE : Raw
th, cat-like response –
f driving miles over wet
the G-800 at your
ow.

G800
SAFETY RADIALS

GOOD⫩YEAR

An advertisement from *Good Motoring* magazine, 1969, extolling the virtues of Goodyear G800 'safety radials'. Standard Minis continued to be fitted with crossplies (the Cooper breed had radials), which were considerably cheaper. Radial tyres had been virtually perfected by 1962 and, apart from giving superior roadholding to crossplies, were also much more durable. The ingenious Dunlop Denovo 'run-flat' tyre – safe up to 50mph when punctured – would arrive in the 1970s, but its relatively high purchase price led to early deflation.

However, during the last years of the Clubman, while Metro prototypes were undergoing tests, the traditional Mini sat quietly confident in the background. Dozens of enthusiasts continued to race and rally Minis, and some were successful, particularly in rallycross. British Leyland clearly saw the writing on the wall for the traditional car, as Volkswagen had for the Beetle at roughly the same time, but no-one in Britain had bargained for the huge impact made by the advent of the classic car movement.

This largely came about in the mid-1970s after the publication of the British journal *Classic Cars*. When the historic rally movement also came into being, largely as a result of the RAC's Golden Jubilee Rally in 1982, interest in the traditional Mini was revived. For this event famous, and not so famous, names dusted off their old rally cars and went out for a spot of serious fun. A number of similar events followed, and enthusiasm for the traditional Mini, particularly the Cooper versions, didn't go unnoticed by British Leyland's top brass.

Towards the end of the 1970s engineers continued to make improvements to the standard road cars, although to all intents and purposes, the car's serious development was long since over.

To celebrate 20 years of the Mini the 1100 Special was launched as a limited edition model in 1979. Two colours were available – metallic silver or metallic rose – and both came with side stripes, matt black radiator grille and a vinyl-clad roof.

The interior of the car was to Clubman specification and had a three-instrument binnacle and comfortable cloth seats. Luxury touches such as a cigarette lighter and radio were fitted as standard. Such was the success of this model – it sold out in a matter of weeks – that it sparked off a plethora of special editions much appreciated by the Mini's most loyal clientele.

The City followed and there was the luxury Mayfair model in 1982. Reviving the name of one of BMC's most famous sports cars, the Sprite appeared towards the end of 1983 and, to honour 25 years of production, the Mini 25 was launched in 1984. Five years later the 30 was launched, and celebrated three decades of Mini production.

By the mid-1980s there were the Ritz, Chelsea, Park Lane and Piccadilly but, despite the appealing colour schemes, body graphics in some cases and luxury interiors, the Mini was still a Mini. While some regarded it as an old friend, there was little to disguise the fact that it was getting extremely long in the tooth.

This aside, there was plenty of life left in the old girl, because at the end of the 1980s, there were developments afoot that would result in the revival of the famous Cooper association with the Mini. Before this 'relaunch', however, there was one special edition that really fired the imagination of motor sport enthusiasts.

English Racing Automobiles

In 1934, ERA produced the first of its A-type voiturette single-seater racing cars. Based on the 'White' Riley these supercharged 6-cylinder cars kept British honours flying throughout the late 1930s, and were highly respected both in Britain and mainland Europe, winning dozens of class, and outright, victories. Naturally, they were no match for the Grand Prix cars from Auto-Union and Daimler-Benz, but nor were contemporaries from Alfa-Romeo and Bugatti, *et al.*

Some 17 ERAs were built all told – they all survive – and continued to be raced after the Second World War, but by the late 1940s were completely outmoded, and gave way to Raymond Mays' exciting, but initially unsuccessful, project at BRM, or British Racing Motors. To many racing fans, the ERA was representative of the archetypal English racing

A new badge appeared in the late 1960s signifying that new masters were in charge of Britain's largest car-manufacturing base. The British Leyland banner embraced a number of marques under one umbrella, but there were too many holes in the canopy to shield them from future storms. That the Mini survived the disaster that British Leyland became is testament to the brilliance of the design.

car, its distinctive radiator badge conjuring up everything that was once great and good about British motor sport – before the great god, television, produced a travelling circus.

The British company Engineering Research and Application Ltd was once involved in the ERA project but, after 1953, its work became more closely associated with Zenith carburettors. The company, and the right to use the ERA name, was passed on to the Jack Knight concern in the mid-1980s, and after a short gestation period the ERA Mini Turbo was announced, officially appearing in 1989.

By any standards it was a most exciting machine, both visually and from behind the steering wheel. ERA badges adorning the 5-spoke alloy wheels and smart matt black radiator grille gave notice of special performance, while the flared wheel arches, deep chin spoiler, twin spotlamps and bonnet 'bulge', tinted window glass and lowered suspension resulted in the production of a classic among classics. (Picture, page 68)

This was a Mini for 'grown-ups' that came with a hefty price tag and performance aplenty from the reworked 1275cc engine. Fitted with a Garrett T3 turbocharger the ERA Mini produced no less than 96bhp at 6130rpm. Top speed was in the region of 110mph, and there was a 0–60mph capability of 7.7secs, which was comparable with the 1.6-litre atmospherically aspirated Mk1 Volkswagen Golf GTi, a hot hatchback that also boasted a top speed of 110mph. Fewer than 380 examples were built all told and, predictably, the majority were quickly snapped up by Japanese enthusiasts who regarded the ERA as the most exciting of the production Mini brigade.

Largely thanks to the popularity of the growing classic car movement, interest in the Mini worldwide was never greater than at the beginning of the 1990s. Throughout the 1980s the long line of special-edition Minis had hinted strongly that the car's final demise was just around the corner, but this was not to be. The Cooper version was revived and once again it appeared that the Mini's future was not only assured but extremely bright.

The British Open

In the summer of 1991 Rover, as it then was, introduced a most handsome cabriolet version. There was nothing new in the idea of a cabriolet – specialist conversion companies (and private individuals) had been producing these in small numbers for many years – but this was the first official 'ragtop' and much appreciated by fans of fresh air and personal invasion by the entomological world.

The car was a 'copy' of the conversion produced by a German Rover dealer (Lamm) on cars, to Cooper specification, supplied directly from the Longbridge factory. Unlike so many home-made specials, the cabriolet had a specially strengthened body to compensate for the loss of torsional rigidity that is inherent in most roofless cars.

Externally the car had wide wheelarch extensions, a chin spoiler, extended rear valance and attractive multi-spoke alloy wheels. A 'full-width' dashboard, sports steering wheel and bucket seats with integral head restraints characterised the comfortable interior.

The cabriolet was accorded instant classic status, a collectors' item for its looks alone. But it was also a practical 'ragtop' and among the most inexpensive to buy. Purists, however, considered the 'tin-top' as the true classic, and throughout the 1990s bought Coopers in particular in ever-increasing numbers.

e Clubman's front end was longer than the traditional Mini's, the sheet metalwork completely enclosing the cular headlamps. The estate's rear was arguably able to balance the nose more effectively than the standard oon's.

For many the Clubman's conventional instrument binnacle, placed in front of the driver instead of in the centre of the dashboard, was fresh, modern and welcome. For dyed-in-the-wool enthusiasts, however, it was uncomfortably close to convention, a concept that, like those in the Volkswagen fraternity, Mini folk more or less eschewed. In much the same manner as British Leyland's management, the needle on the speedometer went round in a circle before returning to zero.

Apeing rally car practice, the owner of this Clubman has concealed Roy Haynes's restyling exercise with fo
extremely large spotlamps. From a practical point of view the additional lighting is invaluable, as standa
illumination was never one of the car's brightest assets. In recent times spotlamps have gone out of fashic
although there is a class of motoring 'reptile' – the type that wear sunglasses at night – who switch on th
foglamps during daylight irrespective of weather conditions.

The popular pick-up truck, wholly devoid of non-essential 'frills', was not subjected to the Clubman
styling, and soldiered on in its usual, quiet way throughout the 1970s. That enthusiasts have
taken to restoring these vehicles in recent times is indicative of the fledgling, but rapidly
expanding, movement devoted to the preservation of classic commercial vehicles of all types.

Although gone by the beginning of the 1970s, the fantastic little Coopers were far from forgotten. In their time British Leyland dropped more clangers than a group of inebriated campanologists, and axing the Cooper S was among them. Twenty years after the car was dropped from the range, a new, but similar version was brought back by Rover, and thousands of Mini devotees gave thanks.

British Leyland introduced the 1275GT Clubman in 1969. Similar to the Cooper S – and built alongside it – developed 60bhp at 5250rpm and boasted a top speed of around 88mph. The Cooper S was faster, argua[b]ly better looking and the choice of sporting purists, but many believed that it was getting long of tooth. Wh[en] Cooper S production finished with the Mk3 version in the summer of 1971, the 1275GT was fitted with rub[ber] suspension – the hydrolastic arrangement of yesteryear was never especially popular – and played the role [of] 'spiritual successor' to the illustrious classic it replaced.

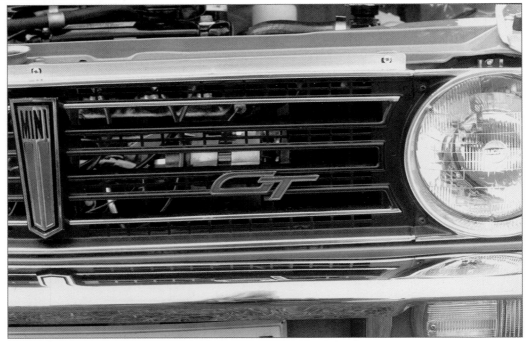

The 1275GT's radiator grille was originally fitted with a vertical Mini badge and GT lettering. Later cars had the Mini lettering placed horizontally in the centre of the grille; the GT badge was discontinued altogether in 1976. This penny-pinching exercise doubtless saved the company money, and pleased the dreary 'men in grey suits' – accountants and other bead counters – but saving pennies at a time when the company was in need of millions made little difference.

Throughout the 1960s the Mini's road wheels were of pressed steel, to a four-bolt fitting and *circular*. There was nothing else to them – no fancy patterns, no 'way-out' 1960s colour schemes – just plain, good ol' circular wheels . . .

. . . and Cooper versions were much the same, only wider and vented.

Stripes and graphics were new phenomena in saloon production during the 1970s, largely started by Porsche of Stuttgart with their 914 (produced from 1969), and lightweight Carrera debuted in 1972. This colourful treatment was partly the result of the bright new world created in the 1960s, and partly because of the influence of sponsorship decals applied to racing cars. The fashion, which had infected even the Volkswagen Beetle by 1973, died within a few years except among Mini owners of the 1990s, who were proud of their classic bonnet stripes and John Cooper signature adorning the bodywork.

A further wheel design from the 1970s, this pressed steel item was painted in silver with black 'highlights' and gave the impression of spoked alloys.

Although it didn't go into production this Safety Research Vehicle was completed in 1974. Special features included a strengthened passenger cell, longer wheelbase and extended, impact-resistant bumpers, all of which are part and parcel of virtually every production car today. Safety in car design had been led by Bela Barenyi of Daimler-Benz since the 1950s; by the mid-1970s, many others in the car industry still had a lot of catching up to do.

One of several Mini-based 'specials', the Hustler, designed by William Towns, was built with a remarkable number of different body styles – 72 all told – for various applications. This example, on display at the British Motor Industry Heritage Trust, Gaydon, has a body made almost entirely of wood. The large glass area gives excellent all-round visibility, but protection from side-impact is compromised.

Despite the many political troubles at British Leyland, and occasional problems over build quality with several models in the range, Mini enthusiasts – and there were hundreds of thousands worldwide – remained loyal. Minis were for driving, enjoying and admiring, despite more modern copies from rival manufacturers that were faster, more comfortable and modern. It was a simple matter of black . . .

. . . and white, with just a few grey areas in between.

erestingly, the Mini acquired a 'cult' following in many European countries, including Germany where the
ular Volkswagen Golf had become a huge best-seller. This Mini was hastily snapped by the author during the
nmer of 2000 in Zuffenhausen, a sleepy suburb of Stuttgart, where Porsche have made cars since 1950. This
ticular Mini, in something of a hurry, was being driven flat-out prior to joining the autobahn, providing a
come breath of air among the massed ranks of Merc and BMW owners.

ring the late 1970s and 1980s a whole host of special edition Minis were launched in an attempt to boost
es. Special editions often indicate the imminent demise of a model but, in the case of the Mini, this wasn't to
The cars continued to roll down the production lines, and many loyal customers kept faith, despite the
ious advantages held by more modern alternatives. Not even the presence of the Mini's intended replacement,
Metro, was enough to convince dyed-in-the-wool Mini fanciers of the error of their ways.

Arguably the most exciting and striking of all special Minis was the ERA turbocharged version, built and and marketed by the Jack Knight concern in 1989. Fitted with a Garret T3 turbo, the 1275cc engine developed an impressive 96bhp at 6130rpm, sufficient for a top speed of 110mph and a 0–60mph best of 7.7secs. This special package included revised suspension, body skirts and spoilers, and attractive wide-rimmed alloy wheels but, regrettably, there were just 380 examples in all and the majority were quickly snapped up by Japanese collectors.

Own many years soft-top versions of the Mini were produced from saloons, by both private owners and specialist conversion companies. Naturally, they varied in quality and, because of the need for strengthening panels at strategic points on the chassis and body, they were burdened with a weight penalty. However, for fans of fresh-air motoring, this didn't matter one jot, because . . .

. . . an empty road on a bright summer's day at the wheel of a 'ragtop' has no equal for devotees of high-speed alfresco motoring – flies-'n'-all. 'Scuttle-shake' over rough road surfaces was present with so many of these cars, and some, but by no means all, rattled themselves into a premature car grave.

An early example of wheel-clamping? As is the case with the Volkswagen Beetle and Transporter, customizers have enjoyed something of a field day with Minis. This 'cut-and-shut' job has resulted in an extraordinarily short wheelbase and two-seater bodywork without doors or roof. Wet-weather handling is not the usual sure-footed Mini experience!

A somewhat neater version of a two-seater cabriolet than the car in the previous picture, this attractive 'notchback' has the advantage of greater boot space but at the inevitable expense of rear passenger seating. Attractive five-spoke alloy wheels and wide arches give aesthetic balance to an individualist's 'ragtop'.

An official Mini cabriolet, from Rover, was late in arriving, making its most welcome debut in the late summer of 1991. The beautiful styling for this 1.3-litre car was similar to the German Lamm Autohaus conversion, and included the chromed radiator grille from the contemporary Mini-Cooper, flared wheelarches and deep front and rear spoilers. Luxury touches included a wood veneer dashboard, stylish white instruments and a padded three-spoke steering wheel. The cabriolet was without doubt a great and welcome addition to the range, but a tad – more than 30 years – late in arriving.

A hand-crafted, 'home-built' cabriolet that, sensibly, incorporates a strong steel rollcage and part of the original roof panel. Leather seats, wooden dashboard, door cappings and steering wheel, plus the scale model atop the dashboard, complete a driving environment with all the classic hallmarks of British taste and eccentricity almost at their best.

In addition to the fabulous cabriolet, Rover revived the famous Mini-Cooper at the beginning of the 1990s. The exciting little car recaptured the spirit of the original gems (covered in the next chapter) to perfection, and wholly revived interest in the British classic. While the fortunes of other models in the Rover range failed to capture public imagination during the dying days of the twentieth century, the Cooper bounced back to success, and fired the imaginations of old and young alike.

3

The Cooper Connection

On the face of it the Mini didn't appear as a car destined for success in competition. In its original 848cc form it was underpowered and, with front-wheel drive, was in contrast to conventional machinery. British saloon car racing at the beginning of the 1960s was dominated by Jaguar; in the 'lesser' classes there were Austin A40s and A35s. Rallying was almost a lottery with successes in international events scored by VW Beetles, Sunbeams, Fords, Mercs and the rest. In some quarters the very suggestion that the Mini, intended as an economy 'shopping' car, could trounce the motoring 'establishment' was an impertinence, and at best, laughable.

Like so many father-and-son business relationships, Charles and John Cooper had their fair share of rows, the severity of which could usually be measured after each by the amount of rubber left on the road outside the family garage by John Cooper's car. Charles was a no-nonsense conservative who called a spade a spade, barged through doors without first turning their handles, and trod warily when it came to spending money. On one famous occasion, son John was speaking to an important client in the United States. When, during the conversation, Charles discovered that he was paying for the phone call – all the way to America – he wrenched the phone from the wall and abruptly terminated the conversation.

In the late 1940s and early 1950s, the Coopers came to the fore with their Formula 3 cars. With simple spaceframe chassis and motorcycle engines mounted behind the driver, the F3 Coopers closely followed the layout of Dr Porsche's pre-war Auto-Union Grand Prix machines. In both 1959 and 1960, the Coopers' mid-engined Grand Prix cars won the Formula 1 Championship with Australian Jack Brabham at the wheel, and finally ended the era in which front-engined racing machinery predominated.

Their cars were relatively simple in construction, cheap to build and extremely effective. It was indicative of Charles Cooper's attitude to car construction, that he invariably referred to Colin Chapman, whose Lotuses were considerably more sophisticated, as 'Flash 'arry'!

John Cooper, however, was a more 'go-ahead' chap, and although Grand Prix fans will forever associate him with his pretty and immensely successful Formula 1 cars, he will arguably be best remembered for his association with the Mini-Coopers.

In the same way that Alpine and Gordini were linked with Renault, Carlo Abarth with Fiat, Schnitzer with BMW and Kremer with Porsche, Cooper became the tuning guru behind the quick Minis. When studying the specification of, or driving, a Cooper today, younger readers will almost inevitably be tempted to wonder what all the excitable fuss was about when the first Coopers became available in the early 1960s. And some will doubtless be minded of the indisputable fact that a modern light-commercial vehicle fitted with a turbocharged diesel engine is capable of greater, or comparable, performance.

However, bear in mind that so many average saloons of the 1960s struggled to reach 65mph, conducted themselves around corners in the fashion of a P&O cross-channel ferry negotiating a harbour wall on a choppy sea, and put many in mind of the relative comfort of a Brookes bicycle saddle!

The Mini-Cooper, first announced in September 1961, was a sporting revelation with performance that belied its appearance and technical specification. In much the same way that Volkswagen's chief executive Heinz Nordhoff refused to support a competition programme for the Beetle, Issigonis was not at first enamoured with the idea of a sporting version of the Mini. Both the German and British machines had been designed as inexpensive 'people's cars', from which racing and rally versions could only distract attention.

Thankfully, John Cooper persisted with his idea for a quick Mini, inspiration for which had come from Mini-engined, single-seater Formula Junior racing cars. It was an eminently tunable little unit, and John Cooper 'breathed' on it in a manner which was reminiscent of the many racing versions of the Austin 7 that were so successful at Brooklands, and elsewhere, during the 1930s.

An artist's impression from 1960 of the excitement of the Monte-Carlo Rally, one of the world's great events, that captured the imagination of everyone with an acute sense of motoring adventure. Many titanic battles, fought high up on the icy roads of the Alps, had passed into rallying legend. The agility and nimbleness of the cheeky Minis, however, would end the amateur spirit of the Monte (and other events throughout Europe), and signal the beginning of increasing professionalism in this demanding branch of the sport.

After the earliest 997cc Mini-Cooper the quick Cooper S was available to members of the public from the spring of 1963. Fitted with the production version of the 1071cc engine there was a maximum of 70bhp at 6000rpm, sufficient for a top speed of 95mph and 0–60mph in 11secs. There were Austin and Morris versions, and choice came down to badge preference.

Disc brakes at the front – these, with chromed hubs, are from a later car – gave the Coopers a huge advantage over many contemporary competition machines that continued well into the 1960s with old-fashioned drums.

Interestingly, John Cooper's idea that a sporting version of the Mini would be a winner was confirmed after 1959 Le Mans winner, Roy Salvadori, drove a Mini to Monza, Italy, in 1959. At the same time that Salvadori left London, Reg Parnell also set sail for Monza in an Aston Martin DB4. Both Parnell and Salvadori were extremely good drivers, with a known propensity for wanting to get a move on. When Salvadori in the Mini arrived ahead of Parnell in the Aston, a Cooper version of the Issigonis masterpiece was almost assured.

The early Coopers differed from the 'cooking' saloons in the most fundamental ways, Cooper having taken the classic tuning route. With a bore and stroke of 62.4mm x 81.3mm engine capacity was increased to 997cc. With a high compression ratio of 9:1, reprofiled camshaft and a brace of SU HS2 carburettors, maximum power output was rated at 55bhp at 6000rpm. Stopping power was taken care of by rear drums and front discs, the latter having been specially developed in collaboration with Lockheed to fit snugly inside the Mini's diminutive wheels.

In a car weighing 1400lbs, engine output was more than adequate to produce a top speed of 85mph, and 0–60mph time of 18.8secs. The benchmark acceleration figure to 60mph, so beloved of journalists down the years, was as irrelevant then as it is now, for what really counted with the Mini-Cooper was its extraordinary ability to keep 'buzzing' at high speed with an experienced driver behind the wheel.

With such relatively little engine power available and such a competent chassis the Cooper could be driven virtually flat to the boards – everywhere! The only facet of the car that compromised its cornering ability was the standard fitment of crossply tyres but, even with these outmoded and thoroughly awful antiquated items, Minis were still capable of outsmarting the majority of their contemporaries.

As an aside the only thing that prevented Coopers from winning more competitions than they did was 'Flash 'arry's' contemporary development of the 1.6-litre twin-cam Lotus-Cortina, which effectively ended the domination in British saloon car racing enjoyed by Jaguar drivers.

The original 997cc Mini-Cooper, or simply the Cooper as it became known, lasted in production as Morris and Austin versions until 1964 when it was replaced by the 998cc version. In the spring of 1963, the Cooper S was debuted and it made an even bigger impression upon an unsuspecting motoring public. It was at this juncture that Britain became gripped in a wave of Mini 'fever' and, after Paddy Hopkirk's overall victory on the 1964 Monte-Carlo Rally, several European motoring enthusiasts were left in head-scratching mode.

The early Cooper S had a reworked and stronger cylinder block, with a stroke of 70.6mm and much wider stroke of 68.3mm to give an overall capacity of 1071cc. Breathing through twin SU carburettors this compact unit developed no less than 70bhp at 6000rpm and 62lb/ft of torque at 4500rpm. Top speed in standard road trim was in the region of 95mph, and the benchmark 60mph figure could be achieved from rest without too much aural discomfort in around 11secs.

The larger engined 1275cc S was available from 1964. With twin SUs and a compression ratio of 9.5:1, it produced 76bhp at 5800rpm, and simply went like stink. A top speed of over 100mph was easily on the cards, and 0–60mph was possible in 10.5secs. Such performance in a small road car had never been seen before; coupled with such squat, good looks and brilliant handling, the Cooper S quickly became one of the most desirable cars of the 1960s.

The Cooper Car Company, based in Surbiton, Surrey, had been extremely successful as constructors of sing
seater racing cars during the 1950s. Their simple methods of construction gave an enviable reliability record, a
two Grand Prix Championships on the trot in 1959 and 1960, with (Sir) Jack Brabham in the driving seat
both occasions. When Cooper turned their hands to Mini tuning, the successes came thick and fast. This Coop
liveried Minivan is on display at the Gaydon museum.

From such a small capacity engine and unassuming car, the Cooper S's performance
was truly astonishing, except to those who closely followed developments in
contemporary Grand Prix racing. Between 1960 and 1966 Formula 1 cars were limited
to an engine capacity of 1.5 litres. Ferrari, BRM, Lotus, Honda, Cooper, Brabham and
others ran with engines developing as much as 200bhp in some cases – astounding
output from an atmospherically aspirated power unit – and, with the benefit of
hindsight, admirably demonstrated the abject folly of modern rulemakers in Formula 1.

Up until the mid-1960s both the Mini-Cooper and Grand Prix machinery in
particular showed perfectly that 'small was beautiful' but, of course, the ancient
Greeks had warned of this more than 2000 years previously!

In the spring of 1964, BMC launched two further models on the Cooper theme,
namely, the 1275 Cooper S and 970cc version of the Cooper S. With its 70.6mm x
81.3mm bore and stroke and 9.5:1 compression ratio, the 1275cc version produced
76bhp at 5800rpm, and 79lb/ft of torque at 3000rpm. By comparison the 970S
produced 65bhp at 6500rom and 55lb/ft of torque at 3500rpm. Because of
changes in rules governing motor sport the 1071cc version of the S was

first major international rallying victory came in 1964 when Paddy Hopkirk and Henry Liddon took 33 EJB
victory. A 1071cc 70bhp car capable of 95mph, that first Monte win caused something of a stir in
international motoring circles, as it just didn't seem possible that a motorised 'shopping basket' could win
thing, let along something as big and important as the Monte-Carlo Rally.

discontinued at the end of 1964, and the 970 Cooper S no longer figured in the
range from January 1965.

Everyone has his or her favourite Cooper S, some citing the shortlived 970 version
as the jewel for its versatility and ability to rev, while others – arguably the majority
– preferred the 1275 for its increased power and speed. Few warmed to the
hydrolastic suspension system fitted from 1964, but the standard fitment of radial
tyres across the Cooper range in the same year provided Mini folk with an even
higher degree of cornering grip.

Radials had been a long time in the making, their development and perfection
having been largely thanks in Germany to Daimler-Benz's chief development
engineer, Rudi Uhlenhaut, and in England by the Herefordshire rally driver Bill
Bengry. In 1962, Bengry was the first to use Pirelli Cinturas in competition, but the
Volkswagen driver experienced a spate of punctures. The tyres 'rolled' on the rims
owing to a manufacturing fault; this was quickly remedied, and the Pirelli Cintura
was eventually relaunched as the Cinturato.

Michelin, Dunlop, Firestone and others all produced their own versions of the
radial tyre, and all without exception were superior to crossplies.

Development of the roadgoing Mini-Coopers generally ran parallel with changes and improvements made to the ordinary Minis. Some exceptions included the additional fuel tank and oil cooler from 1966, which were developments required for homologation purposes on the works competition cars. When in 1967 the Mk2 Mini debuted, Cooper versions were naturally treated to the larger taillamps, 'squared-off' radiator grille and slightly larger rear window.

Choice was between the 998cc and 1275cc cars, the former being discontinued in 1969. The Mk3 version of the 1275 Cooper S debuted in 1970, the principal difference being the presence of conventional 'wind-up' windows in place of the traditional Mini's sliding items. With an increased compression ratio of 9.75:1 there was 76bhp at 6000rpm from these cars. The officially quoted top speed of 97mph, and 0–60mph time of 10.5secs put the Mini-Cooper S – Austin and Morris badges weren't fitted after 1970 – into an elite bracket of sporting saloons.

By comparison, the standard road version of the 1.6-litre Lotus Cortina was capable of a top speed of 105mph, and the 1600cc Volkswagen Beetle introduced in 1970 could manage no more than 80mph. The Cooper S had developed into a motoring legend in its own production lifetime, even for those who had no or little interest in motoring and motor sport. The blockbuster film *The Italian Job* increased the Cooper's reputation as a 'wunderkind', the breathtaking driving sequences, particularly in the sewers of Turin, and hair-raising stunts performed around various parts of the city being carried out by experienced stunt drivers for 'real'. Television broadcasters frequently screen this classic film, and Mini addicts never miss it!

Minis on track

On the face of it the Mini did not make for an ideal competition machine. Over long distances the driving position was uncomfortable, and there simply wasn't sufficient 'grunt' from the diminutive engine. The competition department at Abingdon, Oxfordshire, had long since been used to running 'proper' cars like MGs, which were followed by the big Healeys. When the Mini arrived few took it seriously as a possible rally and circuit contender.

Private owners were the first, therefore, to use the Mini in rallying, the first serious works outing not occurring until a team was entered for the 1960 Monte-Carlo Rally. It was not a happy outing; Dr Sodit, accidents and mechanical maladies all played a part in the event, adding up to a Mini failure.

During the early days of the 1960s, international rallying was a truly great branch of motor sport, indulged by sports men and women. There were works teams serious about winning, of course, but the 'superstar' drivers – Erik Carlsson, Pat Moss, Timo Makinen, Rauno Aaltonen, Vic Elford, Bill Bengry, Paddy Hopkirk and many others of their ilk – were affable, everyday motoring folk whose principal reason for enduring the discomforts of a long rally was simply that they enjoyed the thrill and fun of it. Commercial pressures were largely absent and the cars, even from highly organised works teams, were not so very far removed from standard showroom jobs. Rollcages, 'plumbed-in' fire extinguishers, 'skid-lids' and flameproof overalls were all either derided or hadn't been invented.

This author enjoyed the opportunity of driving the ex-Hopkirk Cooper in the mid-1990s, a great privilege that also proved to be something of an eye-opener. It is virtually taken for granted that modern cars are comfortable and quiet, but easy to forget with the passage of time exactly what 'proper' cars were really like; this grand old Mini is quite the opposite of quiet and comfortable, and made me wonder how Hopkirk and Liddon survived to Dover, let alone the harbour at Monaco.

...thout floor carpeting the 1964 Monte winner's interior is as an unrefined soundbox, every moving mechanical ...mponent vibrating its racket through the sheet metal like a child with a drum kit on Christmas morning. ...orks cars had every conceivable navigator's aid, and a comfortable chair, while Hopkirk made do with a ...ndard seat and sporting wood-rimmed steering wheel.

Before the start of one British national rally, Bill Bengry's navigator insisted on seat belts – rare commodities at the end of the 1950s – being fitted to Bill's Simca. This caused Bill some amusement but, not wishing to lose the services of a good map reader, he duly located and fitted a set of seat belts. Bill's elderly mother peered into the car before Bill set out for the start of the event, and asked what seat belts were for. Bill explained, to which his old mum replied: 'Well, honestly, Bill, if it's going to be that dangerous, I think you ought to stop at home!'

Saabs, Sunbeams, Volvos, MGs, Volkswagens, Rileys, sundry Austins and Ford Zephyr/Zodiacs were among the most popular mounts, but the arrival of the Mini saw a challenge by the BMC 'pretender' to traditional and proven machinery. To some, the Morley brothers' class victory on the 1960 Geneva Rally – the first for a Mini in an international event – was something of a surprise. To those who had witnessed the great Erik Carlsson in the almost equally diminitive two-stroke Saab, also with front-wheel drive, the Mini's ascendance was almost inevitable.

Mini class wins followed on the 1960 Alpine and 1961 Tulip Rallies, but the cars all failed to finish the Monte in 1961. These early outings for the 848cc cars provided the BMC competition department, under the direction of Stuart Turner for 1962, with valuable information about the Mini's strengths and weaknesses. Of these it was clear that agile handling, light weight and engine reliability were on the side of the works team, but that engine power was lacking.

With the 997cc version of Cooper's Formula Junior engine installed, this problem was instantly solved. In rally form this engine produced 70bhp – a mere whimper by comparison with the 600-plus bhp produced by the Group B Audi quattros of the mid-1980s – but this was the early 1960s when motoring life was a little less complex and flustered.

By the time of its debut on the 1962 Monte, the twin-carburettor 997cc Cooper engine was pushing out between 80–90bhp, and although the team had problems on this event, Pat Moss collected the Ladies' prize after her heroic drive in 737 ABL. Stirling's sporting sister went on to take outright victories in the Tulip and German events, with Rauno Aaltonen and Timo Makinen finishing fifth and seventh respectively on the British RAC Rally.

BMC ran a team of 6-cylinder Healey 3000s (producing up to 210bhp) at the same time as the Minis; the Healeys were pukka two-seater sports cars in the best British tradition, and very successful in both rallying and circuit events, but even this powerful machine's performance was eventually eclipsed by the all-conquering Minis.

During 1963 the Mini-Coopers slotted into third and sixth places on the Monte, and Paddy Hopkirk finished second on the Tulip but, after Timo Makinen's fourth place on the 1964 Monte-Carlo Rally, the Cooper finally gave way to the more powerful Cooper S.

The 1071cc S was something of a 'screamer', a beautifully balanced car that almost demanded to be driven hard on the throttle. In Aaltonen's capable hands (and feet), one of these cars won the 1963 Alpine Rally out of the bag. Hopkirk finished a creditable fourth on the RAC, the Irishman scoring the most important victory of his career by taking outright victory on the 1964 Monte-Carlo. This win, arguably above all others, was the start of the Mini's formidable reputation as a 'giant killer' – a David capable of taking on any Goliath and winning.

e famous number 37 1964 Monte winner sits on permanent display at the British Motor Industry Heritage
st at Gaydon today against a background of the Monaco skyline. Luckily, this is one genuine historic car that
n't been 'over-restored'. It is, more or less, in the same condition today as it was when it first saw the light of
. Note the BMC rosette on the front wing.

e of the most evocative motor emblems ever designed, the
C rosette is formally printed with the words 'The British
tor Corporation Ltd'. The heritage, and competition record,
resented by this motif is important to all who recall the days
he Coopers and big Healeys, and many modern-day Coopers
r them in honour of better times long ago.

To prove that the 1964 Monte-Carlo victory wasn't a fluke, or some kind of beginner's luck, Timo Makinen and Paul Easter took AJB 44B to an outright win on the tough 1965 event. On this occasion all crews encountered difficult conditions, including blizzards and drifting snow. Makinen's Mini was the only car on the whole event to reach the finish without incurring a penalty, unlike the three team cars on the 1966 outing which, led by Makinen again, were all disqualified for a wholly insignificant lighting infringement.

However, the 1275S displaced the 1071cc cars within a relatively short period. Few drivers took a liking to the production cars' hydrolastic suspension, but the 1275 won so many rallies, at all levels, that spectators in particular, who warmed to the little cars, didn't give two hoots for the type of suspension system used.

In 1965, the works 1275Ss won seven rounds of the international championship, Aaltonen scoring victories on no fewer than four occasions. The same success followed in 1966, but the season kicked off with the infamous disqualification of the first three cars on the Monte, a travesty of French justice that left a taste of sour grapes for many years ahead. After this debacle Minis won the Circuit of Ireland, Tulip, Alpine, Scottish, Vitava, 1000 Lakes and Munich–Vienna–Budapest, all of which added to the mockery of the Monte result.

It was much the same story in 1967, the year in which the RAC Rally in Britain was cancelled owing to the outbreak of foot-and-mouth, a nasty disease that kills farm animals. For weeks on end, visitors to British farms were compelled to dip their shoes in disinfectant, but happily everything had returned to normal by 1968. For the Minis, however, this year was not particularly successful. There were third, fourth and fifth places on the Monte, and third on the Tulip Rally, but the days of the Mini in top-flight rallying were seriously numbered.

For many competing at national level, and in rallycross, the Cooper S's career was only just beginning. On the international stage, the stakes were vastly increased by

After the farce of the 1966 Monte-Carlo Rally, which, incidentally, was officially won by a Citroën, BMC returned to the little principality in 1967 to settle an old score. On this occasion there was no doubt about the Mini's specification, and Rauno Aaltonen and Henry Liddon took this 1275 car, LBL 6D, to yet another outright victory. This was the last of the truly great BMC victories, as Porsche's 2-litre 911 was on the brink of toppling the Mini from the top spot.

the entrance of the 2-litre Porsche 911. A German sophisticate that by 1967 had been race developed into a potent circuit machine, the 911 also made for an ideal rally car. Its rear weight bias gave it an inherently superior ability to change direction in corners quickly, and unrivalled levels of traction on slippery surfaces. This, in conjunction with 160bhp-plus from its air-cooled, horizontally opposed engine, and typically robust build quality, saw Porsche's rallying fortunes rise rapidly from 1968, and Minis fell behind.

A grey area

The advent of the Mini as a circuit racer was extraordinary, because its specification and mechanical layout were the antithesis of John Cooper's thinking. Cooper had, after all, 're-invented' the mid-engined single-seater in the 1950s, and by the end of this decade had paved the way for rival manufacturers of racing cars to adopt the same configuration. By contrast, the Mini had its engine in the 'wrong' place. Worse . . . it was front-wheel drive!

A number of tuned Minis were campaigned in British club events throughout 1960 and 1961 and lucidly demonstrated that the car's cornering ability, despite the inherent understeering characteristics of front-wheel drive, was something well out of the ordinary.

At this time the vast majority of racing saloon cars were to the traditional front-engined, rear-drive layout, and tuning modifications were by today's standards of a rudimentary nature. Graham Hill, for example, who would go on to win the Le Mans 24 Hours, Indianapolis 500 and Formula 1 championships, began his saloon racing career at the wheel of his old mum's Austin A35 – an almost standard road car which Mrs Hill used as everyday transport during weekdays! And which also proved to be considerably more reliable than Graham's Lotus 16 Grand Prix machine. . .

After Cooper formed a team of works racing Minis which, like the Cooper Grand Prix cars were painted in an evocative shade of dark green highlighted with white stripes, the Mini's potential as a competitive circuit racer was realised. For the whole of the 1960s the Mini-Coopers reigned supreme as class and outright winners in British and European saloon car racing.

For some the Mini provided their first taste of real racing and a stepping stone to higher formulae. Sir John Whitmore, who won the 1961 saloon championship, would go on to prove his talent in Lotus Cortinas. After an illustrious driving career in the 1960s, though, Whitmore moved to America, rejected conventional western ideas and thinking, lost a fortune, returned to British motor sport in the 1980s and demonstrated that spectators had been deprived of one of England's best talents for far too long.

On the other hand Gordon Spice, who took the 1968 British 1000cc championship in a Mini, would go on to gain great success in international sports car racing, both as a driver and constructor. The 1976 Formula 1 Champion, James Hunt, also enjoyed success in a Mini at the beginning of his career . . . until it was discovered that the engine in his car was of greater capacity than those of his fellow competitors. Great character or appalling cheat, no-one can deny that the motor racing world is very much the poorer for his passing.

Warwick Banks, John Rhodes, John Handley and Alex Poole were the principal Mini-driving track heroes during the 1960s, but there were many more.

Down many years saloon car championships have often proved themselves to be the most exciting and competitive forms of motor sport. Great battles in the late 1960s between Escorts, Camaros and Minis have correctly been recorded in legend, but not even the powerful Fords could wholly lay the Mini's career to rest. In theory the little car was outclassed by the end of the 1960s, but a decade later Richard Longman won the RAC Saloon Car Championship's 1300cc class in a 1275GT.

Today, Mini racing is arguably in a healthier state than ever, providing a great forum for motor racing enthusiasts to enjoy track sport almost at its very best. There are, of course, faster, more modern, and cheaper cars in which to go motor racing in the twenty-first century, but for many the Mini holds a special place in sporting folklore – as spectacular and charismatic as ever.

e works successes with Minis in the 1960s inspired a whole generation of enthusiasts down the same road. is 1965 Cooper S, fitted with a non-standard rear-window wiper, is typical of so many cars used in club lying throughout Britain in the 1960s and 1970s. Like the majority of cars prepared for modern 'historic' nts, this Cooper has a non-period rollcage, a most important safety item but still considered namby-pamby by tients' of the old school of motoring philosophy.

The hallmark of a proper rally car, the almost obligatory roof 'candle' was a useful, and oft-seen, part of the 1960s rallying scene. Such accessories were extremely useful, particularly in hilly forest sections, and for reading signposts in the dark but, as night rallying declined during the 1980s, and daytime stage events became popular, roof lighting was no longer necessary.

A 1966 Cooper S with a classic array of four Lucas 'flame-throwers', an arrangement that the majority of cl
rallying people adopted in the 1960s. Note the vintage-style leather straps securing the bonnet and headlamps.

It is worth comparing the spotlamp arrangement in the earlier picture with the works cars
illustrated here. Both 33 EJB and AJB 44B have five additional driving lamps up front – EJB also has
a roof 'candle' – but in very different formations. The pure *son et lumière* evinced by these cars in
their heyday are exactly what historic enthusiasts so successfully recreate on old car rallies today.

A model of simple, but most effective, engineering, the 1275S power unit offered almost endless tuning opportunities beyond the standard production car's 76bhp. Mini devotees are amusingly divided during friendly debates about 'the best Cooper S' engine; the majority appear to prefer the 1275's extra power, while others will tell you that there was nothing like a 'nine seventy' for revving, or a 'ten seventy one' for pulling uphill.

like Paddy Hopkirk's 1964 Monte-winning car, the interior of this Mini, prepared for modern historic events, is omprehensive clutter of equipment, including a fire extinguisher – obligatory under governing regulations – da Tripmaster and non-standard tachometer. One of the most useful changes is the smaller-than-standard eel, which makes the steering feel even more precise and direct.

The author's late father, pictured here in the navigator's seat of Colin Symonds' 970cc Cooper S on the *Heref[ord] Evening News* Rally, 1965. Although a complete devotee of rear-engined German 'tinware', he won more troph[ies] in Minis than any other make of car during the 1960s. The old boy was one of many who considered the 970[cc to] be the 'pick' of all Coopers, but . . .

. . . never complained of the later 1275, which would easily pull well in excess of 110mph on tarmac, or rough for[est] track. And this was, of course, during days when crews rarely wore seat belts, never donned crash helmets, rollca[ge] had hardly been heard of, and flameproof overalls hadn't been invented. Incidentally, winners' prizes comprise[d a] small trophy for the driver and navigator apiece and, if they were very lucky, a gallon of oil for good measure.

Land Rover-like tyres, and a genuine Land Rover component in the form of an electrical plug next to the indicator lens, for quick detachment of the lighting system. This 'tweak' is so typical of the innovation produced by competition, but not one that found its way into production cars.

Every car-crazed kid, and a good many adults, collected models of Mini-Coopers during the 1960s – and still do. One of the most modelled cars of all time, it is a measure of the Mini's enduring appeal and personality that Cooper S miniature die-casts, particularly of the Monte-Carlo rally cars, continue to be as popular as ever among those who can't resist big boys' trinkets.

Identical twins David and Colin Ashton are the proud owners of this sparkling 1965 1275 Cooper S, a completely standard example apart from sporting the optional 4.5J road wheels. Both learned the craft of driving in Minis, and remain completely addicted to its unique characteristics.

young people admiring this Cooper S at a modern car show were born long after the classic sports saloon had
sed in production, but so obviously find the car's charm irresistible. The strong rubber mudflaps attached to
bumper almost became de rigueur on rally cars after the 1968 London-to-Sydney Marathon. This, the longest
the modern car rallies, was won by a Hillman Hunter, an enigma akin to, and as likely as, a Morris Marina
ning the Le Mans 24 Hours. But it happened!

When this Cooper was made, it had become apparent to many that its single fuel tank wasn't big
enough, which is why twin tanks – one each side of the boot – were fitted from 1966. Inevitably, this
change cut down on luggage space, but there was little enough without the additional fuel tank, that
few had real cause to complain. Most were glad of the additional driving range.

As an almost inevitable result of fitting twin fuel tanks, the post-1966 cars had corresponding fuel fillers above the rear lights. This pristine car, pictured at the pretty hillclimb venue of Prescott, Gloucestershire, was built in 1970 close to the end of Cooper production. Its classic white body and black roof, a popular colour scheme on production examples, makes for a refreshing change from the ubiquitous red with a white roof.

A handful of Cooper S owners continue to use their cars in Britain as everyday transport, despite the toll taken by typically awful winter weather, and that breed of motorist (and there are many), who regard supermarket car parks as some kind of automotive assault course. It's also interesting in a classic car market that has witnessed dwindling values since the heady days of the 1980s, that Coopers continue to command sky-high prices, particularly in Japan where they are highly prized.

As a tarmac racer the Mini's long career was most distinguished, particularly during the 1960s when the British Vita team were hurtling their cars around. Smoking tyres, snapping at the heels of Jaguars and many other more powerful cars, saloon car championships came alive and, in contrast to today's touring car spectacle, it was without body contact and broken bumpers flying off!

The achievements of top driver John Rhodes and the British Vita racing team are fully acknowledged on the fuel tank of this late 1990s Mini-Cooper. Five major championships between 1965 and 1968 fully demonstrated the Mini's versatility as a great all-round sporting machine, a car that thrilled spectators and inspired a whole generation to become Mini-mounted.

A Mini contemporary, the Mk1 Lotus Cortina 1600 twin-cam was, with rear-wheel drive, equally spectacular and an outright winner almost out of the box. Although the Cortinas were ahead of the Minis in terms of engine performance, both marques hold fond memories for the many thousands of fans who recall the truly great days – and they really were great – of British and European saloon racing. Historic events are equally worthwhile and should not be missed.

Coopers continue to be raced in a number of championships, including hillclimbs, today. Stripped of superfluous trim, and fitted with wide 'Minilite' alloys – the best wheels for racing Minis – these cars not only look the part, but are also extremely competitive.

...e of the last of the classic Coopers, built in 1971, captured in the paddock at Prescott Hillclimb, 2000. The ...d-summer classic meeting has for many years attracted an oversubscribed entry of many of the great marques, ...d provides an ideal opportunity to study the cars, meet old friends, and soak up a unique atmosphere that ...ply doesn't exist anywhere else.

The Mini's power-to-weight ratio, short wheelbase, traction and easy handling make it ideal for traditional, tight British tracks like Prescott (shown here) and Oulton Park, Cheshire. Many who race Minis today do so on the tightest of budgets, and put every last penny into scraping a car onto a grid, but reckon the effort and sacrifice to be more than worthwhile.

The Mini as a 'giant-killer' depicted in cartoon form, and printed on a T-shirt, one of many 'new' items of clothing that became popular during the 1960s.

The Mk3 version of the Cooper arrived in 1970, and was outwardly similar to the Mk2, but under the skin there was a bigger brake servo and oil cooler. Production of this desirable model ran for roughly 18 months; of the 1,570 Mk3s made, 792 were sold in Britain and 778 were exported abroad. Many mourned its passing, and few Cooper enthusiasts warmed to the styling of the 1275GT that replaced the BMC classic.

With twin SU HS2 carburettors and a compression ratio of 9.75:1, the Mk3 Cooper S developed 76bhp at 6000rpm and 79lb/ft of torque at 3000rpm. In essence, this beautiful 1275cc 4-cylinder unit hadn't changed in many years. Just five years after the demise of the Cooper S, Volkswagen launched the 1.6-litre Golf GTi, a 110mph-missile, which took the concept of the Issigonis masterpiece several steps down the road. And, while the German manufacturer capitalised handsomely on this model, British Leyland went from dismal to disastrous.

Dave Morton and wife Gillian with their concours-winning Cooper S, a car in which Dave passed his driving test in 1986. Despite tempting offers for the car from collectors, they will never part with it because, as Dave comments: 'It is just hysterical to drive. It bounces down the road – you feel every bump – and goes around corners like a go-kart. For its size the car is just so quick.' Mini devotees wholly agree with his sentiments, of course.

A Cooper S at a classic Mini show in 2000 under a tent advertising *The Italian Job*, the famous film of the late 1960s, which did as much, if not more, to advertise the Mini worldwide than the Monte-Carlo Rally victories beteen 1964 and 1967 put together. The antics performed by the Coopers in this classic film were 'for real', but it was typical of BMC that they weren't prepared to offer the film makers any cars at discounted prices, despite the worldwide publicity to be gained.

4

Background noise

Throughout much of the 1980s much of the world had largely forgotten about the Mini and, like this discarded wing, the car quietly stagnated and rotted away. The little car's intended successor the Metro sold well in Britain for a while, but the passage of time showed it to be an unreliable heap with a reputation for rusting, equalled only by its sisters in the range – the Montego and Maestro. Those who bought these cars did so largely out of a sense of loyalty and patriotism in a country that continued to talk about the 'Royal Mint' on the one hand, but a 'National Debt' on the other.

By the 1990s the vast majority of run-of-the-mill, mass-produced motor cars were designed with the Mini's space-, weight- and money-saving layout, with engines mounted transversely in the front driving the front wheels. This trend, started by the Issigonis Mini, held huge production advantages over traditional rear-wheel-drive cars, but it had become clear that the herd had driven the Mini into the background.

Superminis such as the Volkswagen Golf GTi and Peugeot 205 GTi were correctly perceived as spiritual successors to the Mini-Coopers, and became classics in their own right and on merit. Austin-Rover's attempt at competing in this new market resulted in the MG version of the Maestro which, despite its evocative badging, was compromised by poor build quality and a bodyshell with the aesthetics of a corroded biscuit tin.

There was no shortage of inexpensive, economical 'shopping' cars either, this market having been served in abundance by Japanese and German manufacturers. In Britain, Ford and Vauxhall competed year on year for volume sales and Rover, blighted by a dull range of cars with prolific reliability problems and poor image, sank almost into obscurity.

The Mini's intended successor, the Metro, was virtually unheard of outside Britain, and many owners of these cars inside Britain expressed the view that they wished they'd never heard of them either.

All this aside, the traditional Mini was given a new lease of life at the beginning of the 1990s with the 're-launch' of the Cooper. With their evocative colours, bonnet

Despite the deep-seated problems of the British motor industry by the end of the 1980s, there were glimmers of hope for Mini enthusiasts. To celebrate three decades of production, this special 30-year anniversary model was launched, and proudly displayed an appropriate badge on the leading edge of the bonnet. Underneath, it was still a Mini, and devotees appreciated it for what it was – a British masterpiece that had survived a long period of 'political' lunacy.

In 1990, the Mini was given a new lease of life with the introduction of an exciting Cooper version, and the 'old sage' himself gave the project his blessing. John Cooper's signature alone was sufficient to prompt a wave of nostalgia among those brought up on the originals, and awakened an interest in car-mad youngsters caught in the grip of the thriving classic scene. Ironically, the growing classic car movement was initiated and led by Britain.

stripes, multi-spoke alloy wheels in the style of the Minilites of the 1960s and spotlamps mounted above the front bumper, these cars brought back powerful memories of the Mini's competition heyday and they sold extremely well.

Originally fitted with a carburetted 61bhp version of the 1.3-litre engine, these gave way to the 63bhp fuel-injected units but, with catalytic converters finding their way into the exhaust system from 1990 – all new cars were compulsorily fitted with cats from 1992 – power output was artificially low. To many, however, this wasn't particularly significant; Rover and Cooper had provided dyed-in-the-wool Mini enthusiasts with an opportunity to acquire a brand new motoring icon, and the enthusiasts were grateful.

Cooper also brought out an S version with a quick steering rack, competition shock absorbers and stiffened suspension, twin-point fuel injection and tuned exhaust – a unique car among Minis that handled and went like the proverbial dream.

The standard 50bhp Mini was produced concurrently as an alternative to the Metro, but dwindling sales ensured that the car's days were numbered. Despite this an international panel of journalists voted the Mini as The Car of the Century in 1999, a title that is also held by Volkswagen's immortal Beetle, which, incidentally, continues in production at the company's factory in Puebla, Mexico.

'Retromobiles'

During the 1950s and 1960s, a number of car manufacturers created designs – styling masterpieces – that, in the eyes of many, are unlikely to be bettered. During the 1980s and 1990s specialist engineering companies, most notably in Britain,

Whereas the original Cooper had been badged as an Austin or Morris . . .

. . . the new one was a Mini . . .

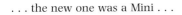

. . . with Cooper badging seemingly everywhere else. This rear view illustrates that the basic package hadn't changed. The lights and bumper were virtually to the same specification as the units fitted upon the introduction of the Mk2 Mini in 1967, but classic touches include the 'quick-release' alloy fuel filler cap, multi-spoke alloy wheels, rally-style mudflaps and bright trim encasing the wheel arches.

created copies of old classics that included C- and D-Type Jaguars, Ford GT40, Porsche RSK and Lola T70 to name but a few.

In the 1990s mainstream manufacturers recognised the true value of this cottage industry, and were inspired to design new cars with 'retro' styling. To this end the Porsche Boxster, BMW Z3 and Mercedes-Benz SLK were all launched with styling touches from the past. All three cars proved hugely successful, and hit a message home to designers that the dreary efforts of the 1980s were not good enough. The car-buying public were truly fed up with bland boxes – and continue to be – but the car industry is rapidly beginning to change. The new Mini, styled along the lines of the original, is surely in response to this change. But this is jumping the gun.

The British *Motoren Werke*

In the mid-1990s Honda ended its association with Rover, the British company passing into the hands of the hugely successful Munich carmaker, BMW. Judged by the unpleasant, and wholly irrelevant, antics of Adolf Hitler some 50 years earlier, the takeover was unpopular with uninformed opinion in Britain. Conversely, BMW's board were initially delighted with their acquisition. They had bought the entire Rover Group, including the potentially lucrative Land-Rover division, for £750 millions, some £250 millions less than the cost of developing the current 5-series BMW!

Within a short time however, BMW's people began to regret getting involved. Rover were in poor shape and for all the usual, familiar reasons. In 1999, exactly 40 years after BMW found themselves heading in the direction of the bankruptcy courts and closure, Rover were in much the same boat.

There are parallels to be drawn between the two companies. BMW got into hot water in the early to mid-1950s because its luxury saloons were stolid, expensive and old fashioned. The inexpensive Isetta 'bubble' cars, launched in 1955, produced little profit, and were largely unwanted after the effects of the 1956 Suez crisis had been laid to rest. The Mini, of course, was also designed as a direct result of Suez, but became rather more successful than the Isettas.

BMW's dire problems, however, were solved in a typically German manner. In the first instance the most important ingredient on the return to success was a massive injection of hard cash from the fabulously wealthy Quandt family. In 1962, the company launched a mid-range 1.5-litre saloon. The car was rushed into production with such severe gearbox and axle problems, that one of BMW's own directors was moved to describe it as 'a shit car'.

This situation was quickly remedied and, over the ensuing years, a range developed into some of Europe's most desirable sporting saloons. In the 1970s, BMW invested heavily in motor sport, in a similar way to Audi in the 1980s. Both German firms are now reaping huge rewards. After Audi's steamroller success – first, second and third places – in the 2000 Le Mans 24 Hours, further success is inevitable.

After BMW finally sold Rover in 2000 – for just 10 quid – the British concern faced, and continues to face, an uphill future. Retired director of Dunlop, Peter Day, who worked closely with the global car industry for many years, is firmly of the view that Rover will survive if it is able to find a business partner prepared to invest heavily in the company.

Superb reproductions of the classic 1960s Minilite wheels were hallmarks of the new Coopers that harked back to the rally and racing days of the 1960s. The centre caps include a laurel wreath in honour of past competition battles and victories. Radial tyres were standard – Pirellis in this case – and gave the car a modern feel. Roadholding and handling were naturally to the same predictably high standard.

In an interview for this book Day commented: 'In the 1970s, industrial relations problems were so bad that investment would have been a waste of time. Quality control was also poor, and in stark contrast to practices exercised in Japanese car factories. In more recent times BMW didn't do a good job of developing new models, and almost killed off Rover's chances of survival by increasing its debts. Now that the company is free of debt, there is a remote chance that it will survive.'

It is interesting that of all models produced under the Rover banner during the 1990s, BMW retained the venerable Mini – the English classic which, even at the beginning of the twenty-first century, close to the end of production, has lost none of its charm.

At the time of going to press, the new Mini has yet to go into series production, although thinly disguised prototypes are being extensively tested on British public roads. English reaction to the new car is predictably mixed. For traditional enthusiasts nothing will ever replace the original car, while others remain stubbornly unable and unwilling to appreciate the subtlety behind creating a brand new car with styling undertones of old. Sceptics, however, will almost certainly be proved wrong in their views.

When Volkswagen unveiled the Concept 1 prototype at the Detroit Motor Show in 1994, and released the production version – the new Beetle – in 1998, a minority of traditional Beetle fans expressed dissent. Some professional commentators also criticised the car; they claimed that the styling was quirky, that the rear of the cabin lacked head and leg room and that it was an ephemeral product of the fashion industry. Some of their criticism was all-too familiar to the Volkswagen 'cult', and

The fuel filler cap on top of the left-hand rear wing is in the classic 1950s and 1960s style, and is held under tension when closed by a simple spring. Small, but important, design features like the Le Mans-style filler are significant marketing tools. German car manufacturer Audi applied the same philosophy to the TT sports machine, which has a 'flush' fuel filler cap in the same style as Group C sports racing cars of the 1980s. Similarly, Volkswagen fit a small flower vase to the dashboard of the new front-engined Beetle, an accessory that all self-respecting VW owners fitted to their classic Beetles in the 1950s.

therefore to be ignored. Volkswagen of America sold 2,500 new Beetles on the day of its official launch and haven't looked back. The car has been similarly successful in Europe. And the critics have all but fallen silent!

The Mini today

Global interest in Minis is arguably greater than at any time in the car's 41 year production history, and continues to make headline news. In 1999, for example, the popular film *The Italian Job* was 're-launched'. At the opening ceremony Sir Michael and Natasha Caine were presented with a special Mini, painted to a design by Natasha Caine. Gold bars were depicted along the flanks of the predominantly black Mini to represent the robbery in Turin around which the film's plot is centred. For many the real point of the film is the presence of Mini-Coopers performing stunts that continue to capture the imagination of all motoring folk with a healthy disregard for the stifling conditions under which most use their motor cars today.

In Britain, parts of mainland Europe and Japan, Minis continue to provide everyday transport for thousands. Apart from being economical they are easy to park, give super performance and are eminently practical. Despite increasing threats to restrict car use, and the spiralling cost of fuel, particularly in Britain, international interest in classic cars is extremely strong. Interest in Minis appears to be growing, particularly among young people who weren't even born when the car was launched.

Throughout the course of the year dozens of Mini clubs organize as many meetings, that are patronised by thousands. In recent times Mini folk have been engaged more and more in the restoration of cars that, under normal circumstances just a few years ago, would have been considered to be beyond economical repair.

Mini enthusiasts are proud of the car's history, and British owners are naturally gratified that this greatly acclaimed car is a product of the once great British motor industry. After BMW's unceremonious 'dumping' of the Rover Group in 2000, and the initial uncertainty over the future role of the British concern, Mini owners in particular voiced their discontent by placing a powerful message on the windows of their cars proudly proclaiming that Minis were '100 per cent free of BMW parts'.

This protest underlined the very strong sentiment which, understandably, still exists for the traditional Mini. But patriotism, however laudable as a concept, is a misplaced concept in the modern car industry. The enormous cost of developing new models has in recent times led to partnerships between the most unlikely bedfellows. The merger between Daimler-Benz and Chrysler, and this new company's takeover in 2000 of Mitsubishi, is a compelling example of the route to the future survival of car producers.

Preserving past glories (and failures) is the concern of museums, such as the British Motor Industry Heritage Trust centre at Gaydon, Warwickshire, a 'Mecca' for Mini fans, and a lasting memorial to the fascinating, and sometimes turbulent, history of British motor manufacturing.

The Mini has become so much a part of motoring lore, that its legacy will live on in the many years ahead. Alec Issigonis died in 1988 at the ripe old age of 81. Production of his greatest piece of work ceased in 2000. Neither will be forgotten.

Plush boot includes carpeted flooring, and a single fuel tank on the left-hand side. Luggage-carrying capacity is as limited as ever, of course, but few really care on the grounds that this is a small price to pay in exchange for enjoyment of the car's finer points.

With these optional wide alloys fitted . . .

there's even less boot space.

As the 1990s wore on the Cooper's interior became more and more sumptuous – a jewel of traditional a quintessentially British design. Top-quality floor carpeting is complemented by a wood veneer facia, leather-c seats and comprehensive instrumentation – all a very far cry from the first production 'Min-bins'.

Placed in a neat row above the radio/cassette player, the volt meter clock and oil pressure gauge are in the same guise as so many classic racing cars from yesteryear. Circular chromed bezels, white faces and black characters provide such a refreshing change to the opposite colour arrangement to be found on so many contemporary cars of the 1990s.

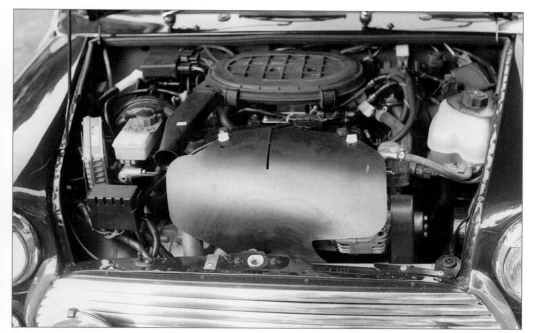

The Cooper's under-bonnet picture is one of a 1.3-litre 4-cylinder engine swamped with fuel-injection equipment, and there's a modern plastic air filter – horrible things that they are – above the rocker box. After many years of Mini owners complaining that their cars occasionally 'die' in wet weather when the electrical system is doused by rainwater, there is also a protective plastic cover over the distributor and sparking plugs.

Developing 65bhp at 5500rpm, the overhead-valve engine's output is strangled by a catalytic converter and other essential emissions equipment, but the trusty unit is basically to the same specification as ever. Major changes include an ECU on the right-hand side of the engine bay (left in the picture) and the water radiator, once mounted on the side, is now in the more traditional place up front. Note the large alternator in the foreground.

Unlike the classic wood-rimmed, alloy-spoked steering wheels of the 1960s, the modern Cooper's is designed to meet current safety regulations. To that end it is a 'chunky', grippy affair with a padded boss, and thumb buttons on the spokes for horn operation. There is no mistaking to which car this wheel belongs, however.

It is worth comparing the interior of this Cooper S, built at the end of original production in the early 1970s with . . .

. . . this 1990s example, which has also been fitted with hip-hugging Cobra, rally-style seats. The interior door panel, window winder and handles are much the same as ever, but there the resemblance ends. A really sumptuous environment in which to enjoy driving, only the narrowness of the cockpit dates the design to the 1950s.

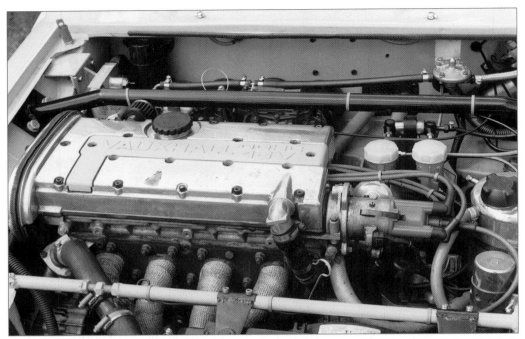

A popular engine conversion among those searching for more power for their Minis, the Vauxhall 16-valve twin cam fits neatly under the front lid. Depending on state of tune, these units can develop as much as 150–170bhp, and easily propel a Min-bin to a top speed in excess of 120mph, but the conversion is not to be advised without uprating the brakes and suspension, and consultation with your insurance broker.

Specially painted in the colours and design of the Union flag, an attractive (to some) and patriotic gesture that demonstrates the pride so many Mini owners have in the 'Britishness' of their cars. Flag-waving, however, is no longer an automatic passport to success in the modern global market, and sentimentality clearly doesn't pay wages.

Like so many 'cult' cars with a following of millions, the Mini lends itself well to the customizer's art and craft. This 1970 example, with wildly flared wheel arches, is just one person's interpretation of creating something unique. The overall effect is not everyone's cup of tea, and one wonders what happened to the Saab 900 that donated the radiator grille, but such cars bring welcome colour to car shows.

There are cheaper and easier ways of acquiring a trailer, but this is one good use for what would otherwise be a dead, rotten, well-rusted and, to all intents and purposes, useless Mini.

A truly long, long piece of equipment, John Hodge once took his home-crafted device to the Goodwood rac
circuit, and discovered, in his words, that it was 'too slow to be interesting'. Apparently, it handles just like a M

MINI LIMO

OFO 678

NEVER UNDERESTIMATE A MINI

it seems likely that it wouldn't be quite so user-friendly on the ice and snow roads of the Monte-Carlo Rally.

With its wide arches, spoked alloy wheels and row of spotlamps, this late example portrays an image of how majority of enthusiasts will remember the Mini in future years . . .

. . . as a 'giant-slayer' that conquered all on the slippery, challenging roads of the Monte-Carlo Rally . . .

. . . and as the diminutive track racer that snapped at the exhaust pipes of Jaguars and Lotus Cortinas during the Mini's fledgling days in the 1960s.

Owners celebrated 40 years of Mini production at a special event at Silverstone in 1999, a great occasion whe
the 'home of British motor racing' played host to thousands of BMC's best. After the euphoria of this spectacul

...ting, the harsh economic reality of the Rover Group was being assessed in Munich by the company's owners, ...W. Simple balance sheets showed dismal news.

The last of the classic Minis was built on 4 October 2000. Similar to this example, this historic car was honoured with a ceremony – an event genuinely mourned by many – but largely ignored by the general news media. After 41 years the old girl was finally pensioned off, but this was by no means the end of the Mini story.

The new Mini-Cooper was officially unveiled at the Paris Motor Show at 12.30pm local time on Thursday September 2000. Scant details, and pictures, of the car were published on the Internet at the same time. Built in UK under BMW's guidance and ownership, Trevor Houghton-Berry, general manager for the Mini in Brit. commented: 'There has been overwhelming demand for information about the new car since it was first announ and this is the best way of reaching a global audience as fast as possible. Many potential Mini customers emb cutting-edge technology and are Internet users, so this is an entirely suitable way to communicate with them.'

Chief designer of the new car, Frank Stephenson, is adamant that it is not a 'retro design car'. His view is that 'it has the genes and many of the characteristics of its predecessor, but is larger, more powerful, more muscular and more exciting than its predecessor.' Mini ancestry is obvious, and there's the added convenience of a hatchback bodyshell.

Profile of the new Mini shows elongated 'breadvan' styling, but attractive interpretation of the classic theme. Opposition to the car in some quarters is typically reactionary; the new Volkswagen Beetle suffered from the same griping and sniping, but spiralling sales figures illustrate that Volkswagen were correct to ignore critics and sceptics.

A fine publicity photograph of the beautifully designed central speedometer tells an interesting story. It is calibrated in kilometres per hour, and not miles, a possible indication that the car will be marketed most strongly on the European mainland.

Sporting a powerful 1.6-litre 16-valve engine driving the front wheels, BMW claim that the new Mini is also the safest car in its class. Modern multi-link suspension, advanced body crumple zones, anti-lock brakes and (up to) six airbags are all part of the specification. Provided that BMW's standard of build quality is adhered to, and the car doesn't develop a typically British reliability record, it cannot fail to succeed. (And will somebody please feed the model!)

e new Mini-Cooper's interior is very much in the modern vogue, with 'retro' touches like the large circular
edometer in the centre of the dashboard. Although it is difficult to appreciate their reasons, some critics have
pressed negative views about the interior styling. In my view, however, it is a laudable attempt to finally bury
e awful, groaning grey plastic that typified so many cars during the 1980s and 1990s. Note that this early
ample is left-hand drive!

Despite the presence of the new Mini, enthusiasts will continue to devote time to the classic Issigonis car that fi appeared in 1959. And beyond the like-minded souls who attend classic meetings for fun, there are the ma thousands . . . (page 128)

Index